DEGENDERING LEADERSHIP IN HIGHER EDUCATION

DEGENDERING LEADERSHIP IN HIGHER EDUCATION

Great Debates in Higher Education is a series of short, accessible books addressing key challenges to and issues in Higher Education, on national and international levels. These books are research informed but debate driven. They are intended to be relevant to a broad spectrum of researchers, students, and administrators in higher education, and are designed to help us unpick and assess the state of higher education systems, policies, and social and economic impacts.

Published titles:

British Universities in the Brexit Moment: Political, Economic and Cultural Implications
Mike Finn

Sexual Violence on Campus: Power-conscious Approaches to Awareness, Prevention, and Response
Chris Linder

Higher Education, Access and Funding: The UK in International Perspective
Edited by Sheila Riddell, Sarah Minty, Elisabet Weedon and Susan Whittaker

Evaluating Scholarship and Research Impact: History, Practices, and Policy Development
Jeffrey W. Alstete, Nicholas J. Beutell and John P. Meyer

Access to Success and Social Mobility through Higher Education: A Curate's Egg?
Edited by Stuart Billingham

The Marketisation of English Higher Education: A Policy Analysis of a Risk-based System
Colin McCaig

Refugees in Higher Education: Debate, Discourse and Practice
Jacqueline Stevenson and Sally Baker

Radicalisation and Counter-radicalisation in Higher Education
Catherine McGlynn and Shaun McDaid

Cultural Journeys in Higher Education: Student Voices and Narratives
Jan Bamford and Lucy Pollard

Perspectives on Access to Higher Education
Sam Broadhead, Rosemarie Davis and Anthony Hudson

Forthcoming titles:

Dissent in the Neoliberal University
Sean Sturm and Steven Turner

Arts and Academia: The Role of the Arts in Civic Universities
Carola Boehm

DEGENDERING LEADERSHIP IN HIGHER EDUCATION

BARRET KATUNA
Sociologists for Women in Society, USA

United Kingdom – North America – Japan – India
Malaysia – China

Emerald Publishing Limited
Howard House, Wagon Lane, Bingley BD16 1WA, UK

First edition 2019

Copyright © Barret Katuna. Published under an exclusive licence.

Reprints and permissions service
Contact: permissions@emeraldinsight.com

No part of this book may be reproduced, stored in a retrieval system, transmitted in any form or by any means electronic, mechanical, photocopying, recording or otherwise without either the prior written permission of the publisher or a licence permitting restricted copying issued in the UK by The Copyright Licensing Agency and in the USA by The Copyright Clearance Center. No responsibility is accepted for the accuracy of information contained in the text, illustrations or advertisements. The opinions expressed in these chapters are not necessarily those of the Author or the publisher.

British Library Cataloguing in Publication Data
A catalogue record for this book is available from the British Library

ISBN: 978-1-83867-133-4 (Print)
ISBN: 978-1-83867-130-3 (E-ISBN)
ISBN: 978-1-83867-132-7 (Epub)

ISOQAR certified Management System, awarded to Emerald for adherence to Environmental standard ISO 14001:2004.

Certificate Number 1985
ISO 14001

INVESTOR IN PEOPLE

To Mom, Dad, Ben, Hans, and Henry for your support and inspiration.

CONTENTS

Acknowledgements xi

1. Introduction 1
2. Effective Academic Leadership 19
3. Learning How to Be an Academic Leader 63
4. Gender and Leadership in Higher Education 109
5. Conclusion, Implications, and Suggestions 149
   Interview Guide 157

References 161

Index 175

ACKNOWLEDGEMENTS

This book is based on my 2014 doctoral dissertation: *Breaking the Glass Ceiling? Gender and Leadership in Higher Education*. Dr Davita Silfen Glasberg chaired my dissertation committee that also included Dr Bandana Purkayastha, Dr Manisha Desai, and Dr Kim Price-Glynn. Each one of them uniquely contributed to this project and guided me every step of the way as I formed my ideas for my dissertation, collected data, and started writing. They helped me to find my own scholarly voice that has led to my theoretical and applied focus on degendering leadership. I am incredibly fortunate to have had mentors at all stages of my academic journey starting at Wyoming Seminary College Preparatory School with Jay Harvey, Mary Ann Hopkins, and Elaine Burg. Then, at Lehigh University, I was significantly inspired and encouraged by Dr Marie-Hélène Chabut, Dr Laura Katz Olson, and Dr Richard K. Matthews. I am also incredibly grateful for such a supportive network of friends and colleagues in the organization I work for, Sociologists for Women in Society, who have cheered me on. A special thank you goes to Dr Christin Munsch of the University of Connecticut who read through the manuscript before my final submission. Other faculty members at the University of Connecticut who have provided exceptional support to me throughout graduate school and my professional career include: Dr Laura Bunyan, Dr Gaye Tuchman, Dr Elizabeth Holzer, Dr Mary Bernstein,

Dr Nancy Naples, Dr Bidya Ranjeet, Dr Daisy Reyes, and Dr Heather Turcotte. Thank you to all of my peers and former colleagues at the University of Connecticut who contributed to my professional journey.

I would not be where I am today without my family including my mother, Joann Brandt, father, Elliot Katuna, and sister, Cara Wagner. My mom is one of the strongest people I know and I am thankful that I have had her strength to rely on. My father has guided me in spirit throughout my professional journey. I initially worked at his barrister's desk during the first part of graduate school and found solace in using this space as a creative environment for me. He died too young to see me graduate from middle school, high school, college, and graduate school. However, I know that he – just like my mom – would be incredibly proud that his youngest daughter is now the sole author of a published book. He only got to see me reach the age of six – but I know that he would be beaming with pride if he could have this book on his bookshelf.

My husband, Benjamin Kehl, and twin five-year-old sons, Hans and Henry, have provided me with support (with a mix of comic relief) that has helped me to focus on completing this book. Being a mother makes me realize how much I want to contribute to this world. I want to contribute ideas that will open doors and possibilities for those who have been historically marginalized. This book will open up leadership opportunities and will limit confining gendered understandings of how one ought to lead based on categorical classifications.

I would also like to acknowledge the 34 study participants who were willing to take time out of their busy and unpredictable schedules to take part in an interview. I am greatly inspired by their experiences. I am thankful that they shared some exceptionally personal stories that add to the richness of my data.

1

INTRODUCTION

It's problematic to use the terms "masculine" or "feminine" to define a leadership style. Even if a university board member applauds a woman's leadership as "masculine" because she is hardheaded and unyielding in her commitment to canonical rules of the institution, it's still problematic. Even if a university dean praises a man's "feminine" presidential leadership because he frequently hosts student office hours, welcomes student leaders into his family's home on campus for dinners that he cooks, and allows others' opinions to guide conversation before jumping in with his perspective, it's still problematic. Critics of the leaders in the aforementioned examples might say, "why can't she lead more like a woman should?" or, "why can't he lead like a man?"

Binary, gendered characterizations lead to a stereotypical framework that reinforces gender essentialism that men and women are wired differently, and loses sight of individual leadership approaches that are likely a combination of personality, intellect, awareness, commitment, and prior experience. Assessing leaders with gender binary glasses also limits opportunities for trans, non-binary, and intersex leadership in higher education. Degendering leadership opens the door for this diversity that institutions should be preparing for.

While women have not yet broken the glass ceiling in academia (Agathangelou & Ling, 2002; Alexander, 2005; Pierce, 2003), they are increasingly joining college and university boards (Brown, 2009) and presiding at some of the most esteemed colleges and universities. From 2011 to 2016, according to the American Council on Education (ACE, 2017b), the percentage of women presidents at institutions of higher education increased from 26.4% to 30.1%. Data published by ACE show that this percentage has steadily climbed since the 1980s. ACE data from 2017 reveal that 5% of all college presidents were women of color (ACE, 2018). Overall, the ACE American President Study 2017 shows that from 2011 to 2016, minority representation among college presidents increased from 13% to 17% (ACE, 2017a). Leaders from different demographic backgrounds with respect to gender, age, race, sexuality, and ethnicity are governing higher educational institutions. They come from different academic disciplines, serve in varying roles at differentially sized institutions, and represent a diverse array of experiences that led them to senior administration.

This book addresses the following questions: (1) What role does gender play in the narratives of women and men leaders? (2) How does gender figure into women and men's descriptions of their workplace interactions? (3) How might leaders' gendering of leadership reproduce gender stereotypes? (4) What strategies might leaders and institutions of higher education use to degender leadership? and (5) What might degendered leadership look like?

Overall, this book demonstrates the power of the narratives of senior higher educational administrators to degender leadership. In this chapter, I define leadership in gender-neutral terms, discuss literature on gendered leadership style variation, and through a feminist degendering movement framework, challenge gendered leadership differentiation. I also introduce my methodological framework and guiding research questions.

Chapter 2 helps us move away from gendered leadership constraints by defining effective academic leadership through both scholarly contributions and the voices of my interview participants that take institutional values and norms, as well as university stakeholder expectations, into account. These conversations will especially inform search committees for university administrators, as well as professors who are looking to advance.

Chapter 3 focuses on the formal and informal trainings and experiences that are the foundation for learning the leadership skillset and that will be the basis for a successful career in higher educational administration. I note the relevance and potential limitations of gender-specific trainings for women leaders in this chapter.

Chapter 4 addresses respondents' reactions to the socially constructed masculine versus feminine leadership framework as well as instances in which respondents felt that gender mattered, or did not matter, with regard to their work. This discussion demonstrates the need to disentangle gender and leadership so that administrators can lead without underlying expectations.

Chapter 5 concludes that gender identity does not predict leadership style. Reported leadership styles did not vary among my diverse sample of interview participants with respect to gender. University leaders, from a variety of gender, racial and ethnic, disciplinary, geographic, institutional, and administrative backgrounds reported leading in very similar ways. I discuss the larger implications of these findings in my conclusion that speaks to the future of university inclusivity that starts from the top down.

I went to the top of the university hierarchy to learn about how leaders really operate. Popular self-help books and media discourse have framed a message that women leaders need to develop masculine survival skills to thrive in a "man's world." Had women leaders in academic settings actually bought into this? Did men serving as deans, provosts, and presidents, really have a different playbook? My findings dispel these gender essentialist messages.

THEORIZING LEADERSHIP VARIATION

Lorber's (1994, 2000, 2005) "feminist degendering movement" acknowledges the fluidity and malleability of gender and Butler's (2004) notion of "undoing gender" that calls to reduce the power of gender as an organizing principle, inform this "trait degendering" focus. Degendering leadership dismantles preconceptions, stereotypes, and hierarchies. We live in a society in which we are highly familiar with a gendered, social construction of leadership (Brescoll, 2011; Eagly & Carli, 2007; Koenig, Eagly, Mitchell, & Ristikari, 2011). External responses to leadership are oftentimes rooted in a leader's gender identity and gender roles embedded in all social institutions.

Leadership scholars have synthesized style classifications that cover a variety of leadership manifestations. Lewin and Lippitt (1938) introduced the polar opposites of democratic and autocratic leadership styles that other leadership scholars (e.g., Eagly & Johannesen-Schmidt, 2001; Eagly, Johannesen-Schmidt, & van Engen, 2003; Eagly & Johnson, 1990) have built upon in their efforts to characterize gendered leadership variation. Notably, Eagly and Johnson (1990) do not find differences in how women and men approach the social and instrumental factors associated with leading. However, they find that women are more open to collaborative, democratic leadership styles. Women avoid an autocratic leadership style since operating in such a way can lead to intense scrutiny and personal repercussions. Social role theory explains why women develop this democratic leadership style; stereotypes regarding a woman's role in society prevent her from acting in an autocratic fashion. Openness and transparency in women's decision-making as leaders is therefore attributable to gender roles. Women are not biologically wired differently to be collaborative; social norms oblige this leadership style. My research confirms that women avoid an overly autocratic leadership style. Yet, my research challenges this understanding because men also avoid such a domineering presence.

More precisely, leadership scholars have identified a variety of leadership models that are often dichotomously used to define gendered leadership including shared governance and collaboration, communal versus agentic leadership, transactional versus transformational leadership, and a laissez-faire approach to leadership. I contend, through my findings, that these definitions are to be viewed as multidimensional representations of leadership where all leaders, regardless of gender identity, situationally shift between styles.

A shared governance model emphasizes the importance of collaborative involvement of faculty and pertinent institutional stakeholders and is marked by transparency, democratic engagement, and equal opportunities for individuals, at all levels, to weigh in on significant prospects for institutional change. Open deliberation is the mark of the shared governance model and the culture of higher education warrants this framework. Sometimes institutional figureheads are fairly new to an institution when major decisions are in store and it is important, for example, that prominent stakeholders with historical university roots, feel like their opinions matter. Leaders with long tenures in academia generally buy into this shared governance model and shy away from any autocratic decisions, unless emergency situations warrant swift action.

Communal leadership emphasizes power sharing, whereas an agentic style incorporates assertive independence (Bass, 1990; Cann & Siegfried, 1990). Communal leadership involves more than decision-making based matters, as is the case with democratic leadership, by incorporating a sense of oneness among the stakeholder community. Furthermore, agentic leadership differs from autocratic leadership given that leaders can be assertive and independent without necessarily wielding single-handed decisions. Scholars underscore societal expectations that women will exhibit a more communal, or collective/community-related leadership approach, while men are expected to have a more agentic approach that is marked by independence in decision-making (Eagly & Carli, 2007; Koenig et al., 2011; Spence & Buckner, 2000). Eagly and Carli (2007, p. 123) find that, "… [women] have to reconcile the communal qualities that people prefer in women with the agentic qualities that people think leaders need to exhibit to succeed." Exhibiting too much communality or too much agency could damage a woman leader's reputation.

Gendered democratic/authoritarian and communal/agentic leadership styles are in part related to the dichotomy of *laissez-faire* versus *hands-on* styles. Studies show that men were more likely than women to exhibit a laissez-faire style (Eagly et al., 2003) that is marked by a hands-off approach likely resulting in inept management (Bass, 1990). This leadership style is rooted in social role theory and gender roles.

Other comparisons are characterized in terms of transactional and transformational leadership. A transactional approach, characterized by micromanaging with careful monitoring of worker responsibilities, differs from transformational leadership that is more team oriented and involves goal setting and mentoring from above (Bass, 1998; Burns, 1978). Eagly and Carli (2007) find that the transformational approach is the most effective leadership style and that women most commonly exhibit this leadership style: "at least one aspect of transformational leadership is culturally feminine – *individualized consideration*, which is consistent with the cultural norm that women be caring, supportive, and considerate" (p. 130) and perform considerable "emotional labor" in their leadership to acknowledge the views and sentiments of fellow stakeholders in both the best and worst of circumstances (Hochschild, 1983).

Given what we know about leadership practices and styles, finding out how leadership *actually* operated in the higher echelons of academia meant securing interviews with some of the most scheduled and visible figures in university leadership. I next discuss my study design and interview strategy.

STUDY DESIGN

I used a feminist interview strategy with a semi-structured interview schedule to address participants' power structure negotiations. Mechanisms for climbing an organizational ladder that they may have adopted at much earlier stages in their careers (Chase, 1995) may not have become evident via a fixed schedule that did not allow for flexibility and the establishment of rapport in the interview relationship (Sprague, 2005).

Through life history/oral narrative interviews (DeVault, 1999; Naples, 2003; Smith, 1987), I learned about the "relations of ruling" (Smith, 1987) that structured these leaders' experiences. First, I prompted the participants to begin with a story of how they became interested in institutional leadership and, through this approach, I was able to make sense of their career pathways. This revealed participants' relationships with mentors who may have promoted leadership advancement and how this relationship may or may not have been reinforced by a gendered, raced, or classed institutional structure.

Between February 2013 and August 2013, I interviewed 11 deans, 12 presidents, and 11 provosts (18 women and 16 men) for a total of 34 interviews, each lasting between 30 minutes to 2 hours. All respondents were cisgender men and women. Two of the men are from historically marginalized racial and ethnic populations in the United States. Three of the women I interviewed were women of color and one of the women was white and from a Western European country. One of the women was a white, openly out lesbian. None of the men that I interviewed identified as gay. The lack of diversity with regard to race and sexuality is reflective of the lack of diversity in the power elite within the United States. Yet, the power elite, that was once reserved for white men of privilege (Mills, 1956), is more diverse today than it was when Mills first wrote about it in 1956. Zwiegenhaft and Domhoff (2006) argue that people of color and people from other marginalized social locations, both men and women, are taking on leadership roles in political, corporate, and academic spheres through election, nomination, and appointment. While this may be the case, underlying vestiges of racism, sexism, and homophobia from within the academy create boundaries for many academics who do not fit the white male paradigm that has historically marked the academy (Alexander, 2005; Davis, 2005; Pierce, 2003; Williams, 1991). This book is in direct response to this need for leadership diversity in all institutions; degendering leadership holds the promise for continued gains in leadership diversity.

Overall, my interviews were with leaders from a total of 17 different institutions. Seventeen of the interviews were with academic leaders from private institutions, including five deans, eight presidents, and four provosts. An additional 17 of the interviews were with academic leaders from public institutions, including six deans, seven provosts, and four presidents. Since patriarchy is often an underlying feature of religious institutions, I did not interview any leaders presently residing at religiously affiliated institutions (Chong, 2006). I also chose not to interview any academic leaders from military institutions or all-women's institutions. Patriarchal origins of the United States military mean a significantly lower likelihood that women would hold positions of authority there (Archer, 2013). I did not interview leaders from all-women's institutions because such colleges are often settings where women are disproportionately advantaged in terms of leadership advancement opportunities (Langdon, 2001). Eliminating these variables from my sample helped me to hone in on leadership where these unique circumstances are absent and contributes to the generalizability of my research to other settings.

Since I was most interested in seeing responses to a diminishing system of patriarchy, I chose to focus on universities and colleges that have a solid commitment to diversity among their recruitment of faculty, administrators, and students. I determined an institution's commitment to gender diversity through its level of support for women in the science, technology, engineering, and math (STEM) fields. The host institutions of the men and women that I interviewed had a history of STEM-related programing on their campus. Some of the institutions either had or had applied for an ADVANCE grant from the National Science Foundation that is for the purposes of increasing the participation and advancement of women in academic and science and engineering careers.

Geographically, within the United States, I had representation from the Mid-Atlantic (MidAt), New England (NE), Midwest, and West Coast (WC). The MidAt representation included five presidents, two provosts, and one dean. One president was from a Midwestern university and one dean was from a university on the WC. The remaining university leaders were from NE, including nine deans, six presidents, and nine provosts. In addition to in-person interviews, I relied on five video calls, via Skype, and one traditional phone call without video for my data collection.

Of the 34 respondents, 28 had terminal degrees in a discipline that is often housed within a university's College of Arts and Science (e.g., political science, English, psychology). Two of these respondents did not have doctorates, but a terminal degree in their discipline. Of the remaining six respondents, one had a doctorate of education, two had doctorates in business, and three had doctorates in engineering. Since I relied on snowball sampling and worked through the various networks in which I am a member to gain access, I was not able to ensure disciplinary diversity. Disciplinary homes were often more relevant to respondents' stories of their pathways to leadership. For example, since women are more commonly professors within Colleges of Arts and Science than in Colleges of Engineering (Bird, 2011; Fox, 2010), differential gendered dynamics mark these experiences. For this reason, I do consider the disciplinary home of the leaders in my analysis. However, to protect the identity of the interview participants, I do not specifically mention the participants' exact disciplinary focus. I use the four categories of: Arts and Sciences (A&S), Business, Education, and Engineering (Eng.).

Pseudonym	Discipline	Race/Ethnicity	Region	Type	Role	Gender
Sabrina	A&S	Latina	NE	Public	President	Woman
Maria	A&S	White	WC	Public	Dean	Woman
William	A&S	White	NE	Public	Dean	Man
Candace	A&S	Latina	NE	Public	Dean	Woman
Ronald	A&S	White	NE	Public	President	Man
Emily	A&S	White	NE	Public	Provost	Woman
Joanne	A&S	White	MidAt	Private	Provost	Woman
Eugene	Business	Arabic	NE	Public	Dean	Man
Anna	A&S	White	NE	Public	Provost	Woman
Sophia	A&S	White	NE	Private	Provost	Woman
Jake	A&S	White	NE	Private	Provost	Man
Gina	A&S	White	NE	Public	Dean	Woman
Louis	A&S	White	NE	Public	Provost	Man
Bradford	A&S	White	NE	Private	Dean	Man
Steven	Eng.	Asian	NE	Public	Provost	Man
Matthew	A&S	White	NE	Private	Dean	Man
Paul	A&S	White	MidAt	Private	President	Man

(*Continued*)

Pseudonym	Discipline	Race/Ethnicity	Region	Type	Role	Gender
Douglas	A&S	White	NE	Public	President	Man
Samuel	A&S	White	NE	Private	Dean	Man
Corinne	A&S	White	NE	Private	Provost	Woman
Cynthia	A&S	White	MidAt	Private	Dean	Woman
Nadine	A&S	White	Midwest	Private	President	Woman
Isabella	A&S	White	NE	Public	Provost	Woman
Stanley	Business	White	NE	Public	Dean	Man
Nicholas	A&S	White	NE	Private	President	Man
Christopher	Education	White	MidAt	Private	President	Man
Laura	A&S	White	MidAt	Private	President	Woman
Lisa	Eng.	White	NE	Private	Dean	Woman
Frederick	A&S	White	NE	Private	President	Man
Rachel	A&S	Black	NE	Public	Provost	Woman
Denise	A&S	White	MidAt	Private	President	Woman
Stella	Eng.	White	MidAt	Private	President	Woman
Caroline	A&S	White	NE	Public	President	Woman
Marcus	A&S	White	MidAt	Public	Provost	Man

I adopted a reflective practice to identify the hidden biases and preconceptions that I may have brought to the interviews. While my questions served to guide the course of the interview, I inevitably became the instrument for analyzing these interviews. As such, I mitigated my power as the interviewer/data analyst (Harding, 1986; Martin, 2001; Naples, 2003). By considering the way in which my own life history prompted me to explore gender and leadership, I was able to better assess my relationship to the project. For example, the personal revelation that my purpose is related to identifying binary, socially constructed assumptions that place women and men in fixed categories of acceptable leadership styles positioned me to be exceptionally attuned to probing for life history accounts that are driven by essentialist gender categorization. I also understood that essentialist references may have been research participants' coping strategies for navigating a diverse academic environment.

Once I completed the interviews I employed a standpoint epistemological, or "a sociology for people" (Smith, 2005, p. 10) approach that allows for lived experiences to guide ethnomethodological knowledge discovery (DeVault, 1990; Naples, 2003, Pascale, 2007; Smith, 1987; 2005; Sprague, 2005). Knowledge production can never be complete given variant social experiences based on social differences including race, class, gender, and sexuality (Naples, 2003; Pascale, 2007). This approach comes out of a feminist tradition that has viewed discourse as constraining to those of historically oppressed populations. According to DeVault (1999, p. 59), "language itself reflects male experiences, and […] its categories are often incongruent with women's lives." Instead of insisting that gender matters, I explored the role that gender plays given subjects' responses. While I did ask one pointed question regarding gender-related experiences of an academic leader, using a grounded theory approach (Glaser & Strauss, 1967),

I allowed the themes relative to gender and leadership to emerge without insisting on this connection.

Through discourse analysis, I recognized that narratives cannot only be taken at face value (Chase, 1995; Naples, 2003). Gendered, raced, and classed realizations of oppression may not always be visible to individuals who are not accustomed to this language and who might have been socialized not to see or focus on their oppression (DeVault, 1999). Hidden power dimensions are a key feature of any organizational context (Acker, 2006; Britton, 1997, 2000); therefore, I accounted for the latent meanings that may have been present in my respondents' narratives. By listening to not only what respondents said, but also how they said it, I facilitated the incorporation of unstated meanings into my data. For example, how a leader spoke about a man who mentored her (with a tone of admiration and respect) and about a woman who mentored her (with a tone reminiscent of collaborative friendship) are data that I was able to discern through discourse analysis.

A feminist standpoint epistemological guiding lens for inquiry is not completely absent of potential bias. I mitigated this subjectivity by journaling my pre- and post-interview impressions and emotions (Naples, 2003; Sprague, 2005). Before each interview, I would prepare by reviewing the available background information on the respondent and would account for any prior assumptions that may have influenced the data. While reflective practice throughout the research process has the potential to diminish biases, reflective practice does not diminish personal ideologies (Naples, 2003). I maintained objectivity through mentors who advised me on this project as well as my commitment to remaining true to my respondents' intentions given the high likelihood that these academics would likely read this published research.

LEADERSHIP STYLES AND GENDER

How does gender factor into leadership style? While women and men may offer different gender-specific leadership styles and strategies, these distinctions are often translated into essentialized expectations for how leaders *must* execute their responsibilities. These classifications thus reinforce the social construction of leadership as a gendered phenomenon.

Gender as an organizing principle patterns our interactions in organizational contexts as it operates in other domains of society. Ridgeway (2001, p. 644) asserts that in workplace and organizational settings, gender offers an "implicit, background identity" that frames women and men's responses when they are in command. In what circumstances is gender visible in organizations? Butler (1990, p. 180) points to the process by which gender operates in organizational contexts, noting that, "gender reality is created through sustained social performances." As such, women, who have historically been relegated to private sphere, non-hierarchical positions that require taking orders instead of giving orders, may shape their leadership styles in such a way that they are communal, democratic, transformational, and transactional with regard to acknowledging and rewarding exceptional practices among subordinates.

Social role theory offers one theoretical explanation of differential gendered leadership[1] (Eagly, 1987; Eagly & Johannesen-Schmidt, 2001; Eagly et al., 2003; Eagly & Johnson, 1990; Eagly & Karau, 2002). From this perspective, "leaders occupy roles defined by their specific position in a hierarchy and simultaneously function under the constraints of their gender roles" (Eagly et al., 2003, p. 572). For example, Keohane (2010) underscored how Judith Rodin, former president of the University of Pennsylvania, justified her interest in revitalizing the surrounding Philadelphia neighborhood as rooted in her status as a woman and mother. Keohane (2010, p. 132) explains this style: "Some women may emphasize their stereotypically feminine qualities to make their colleagues, superiors, and subordinates feel more comfortable with their leadership." I found the opposite situation to be true. Women leaders did not commonly underscore their feminine qualities with their peers or their roles as mothers in their discourse. While these matters were certainly not absent from their experiences, they were simply not a focal point that women leaders emphasized. This did not mean that women hid their femininity or subscribed to the understanding that they must wipe all non-masculine items from their professional lives. Caroline, the president of a public university, drew attention to a sports-themed Barbie that sat on her office book shelf and Rachel, the provost at a public university, mentioned that her cell phone cover is pink.

In campaign politics, it is more likely for candidates to play on purported strengths associated with their gender identity. Michele Bachelet's first candidacy for President of Chile in 2005 incorporated a binary understanding of feminine versus masculine leadership. Bachelet succeeded in winning the presidency by relying on a political platform that emphasized what she referred to as "*'liderazgo feminino'* (feminine leadership)" (Thomas, 2011, p. 65). She invoked rhetoric that acknowledged her difference in leadership style that was more inclusive of popular interests and that was an alternative to the sexism and masculine leadership styles that had historically pervaded Chilean politics. Bachelet's strategy developed as a result of the ways in which her two male opponents framed their leadership styles in opposition to her style. Thomas (2011, p. 65) points out that Bachelet's opponents "emphasized a type of political leadership that depended on specific understandings of men, masculinity and politics to simultaneously present their qualifications and to critique Bachelet's." The presidential campaign became a battle between a masculine leadership style and a feminine leadership style. Thomas (2011) writes:

> *She [Bachelet] further claimed that while strength, honesty and conviction do not have a gender, her experiences as a woman meant that she brought a different perspective into politics, a perspective that had been excluded. (p. 76)*

While it is certainly noteworthy that Bachelet deflected masculine understandings of leadership (that have traditionally limited women's access to positions of leadership) by replacing them with feminine leadership, this approach is problematic as a long-term strategy for women's leadership advancement. The feminine leadership approach will not appeal to all women who are running for political office. Furthermore, we are in a position to see more trans, non-binary, and intersex candidates running for office and these candidates would likely find this strategy problematic.

Some scholarship (e.g., Book, 2000; Dunlap & Schmuck, 1995; Helgesen, 1990; Rosenthal, 1998) finds that pointing out women's differential leadership approaches is uniquely feminist and subsequently points to women's exceptional capacity to lead. Institutions will oftentimes celebrate first women leaders. Yet, I do not support this polarizing line of thought that implies gender essentialisms. It is perfectly fine to acknowledge great historical achievement, but the conversation needs to stop with the celebration of gender diversity to allow individuals the space to lead absent gendered assumptions.

Studies indicate that women leaders may demonstrate leadership approaches that are different from men's leadership styles. Yet, it is not gender essentialist to report these findings because they explain why women may have developed these tactics as a result of differential social experiences. Fueled by gender stereotypes and societal pressures, women have learned to cope within contexts that were not traditionally open to them. The fault in the gendering of leadership lies in the prescriptions and definitive assertions that are evident in leadership characterizations that are exclusively rooted in gender. The trait gendering of leadership significantly affects women's workplace advancement as well as the workplace advancement from within the trans, non-binary, and intersex community in all social institutions.

NOTE

1. Eagly and Karau (2002) introduce role congruity theory of prejudice that evolves from and extends social role theory and establishes a framework for future studies of prejudice.

2

EFFECTIVE ACADEMIC LEADERSHIP

Interviews with some of the most highly visible and noteworthy academic administrators in the United States helped me develop a working definition of effective academic leadership that moves away from gendered constraints that may socially and culturally characterize how leaders ought to approach their administrative roles. Academic leaders, much like corporate and governmental leaders, must be equipped to swiftly respond to changing circumstances that affect a university community. Just as leaders ought to be capable of envisioning innovative directions in research and instruction when it's business as usual on campus, they must also be prepared and ready to adapt and respond to a volatile market, campus-wide emergencies that can have safety implications, and publicly controversial situations. Conversations in this chapter will especially inform search committees for university administrators as well as professors considering academic leadership.

Effective leadership incorporates communality, shared governance, teamwork, and proper rewards and acknowledgements for exceptional performance. But, beyond these components that offer a general frame for effective leadership, there are multiple other key ingredients that are essential for academic leaders that include: (1) exceptional academic credentials (Goodall, 2009); (2) leading with a strong ego, not a big ego that incorporates sincere care for the institution including (a) respect for the institution's established culture, (b) caring first about the institution and its long-term well-being (Budig, 2002), (c) support for the work of others (Rowley, 1997) that means valuing a diversity of opinions, and (d) teamwork and credit sharing for collaborative work (Buller, 2011; Jones, Lefoe, Harvey, & Ryland, 2012); and (3) transparency in institutional procedures (Jaradat, 2013; Mahoney, 1998; van Ameijde, Nelson, Billsberry, & van Meurs, 2009). This chapter focuses on what makes an effective academic leader given an institution's overall values and culture that characterize what institutional stakeholders hold in high esteem in the selection process of academic leaders, in addition to all of these aforementioned key ingredients.

EXCEPTIONAL ACADEMIC CREDENTIALS

In most cases, academic administrators, serving in the role of president, provost, or dean, are expected to hold a terminal degree, usually a doctorate, in their specialty. Goodall (2009) argues that there is a relationship between the ability to lead a research university and level of scholarship. Tuchman (2009) attests to the lack of respect that faculty at a research university have for what she terms "corporate administrators" who are incoming outside administrators with lackluster publication records. It is highly noticed when top administrators are evaluating faculty based on research criteria that they, themselves, could not live up to. When faculty members perceive that their accomplishments far outweigh those of their superiors who are telling them to "publish or perish," it is no wonder that a weakening of respect, which Tuchman (2009) witnessed, may occur. My respondents emphasized the importance of academic excellence in the classroom, through teaching,[1] and in the discipline, through peer-reviewed publications. In some cases where a mention of a scholarly track record did not explicitly evolve from the respondents' insights, the fact that they had established and sustained their reputations within their disciplines suggested that a respectable scholarly record is a presumed qualification for leadership. For some of my respondents, current disciplinary-related research projects were still in progress. However, the 24/7 demands of university leadership often meant slow progress, publications based on past data collection, or collaborations. The respondents who did speak of current research projects were not in their prime years of research productivity. It was likely that a combination of their productivity and visibility within their disciplines was a stepping-stone to their academic leadership posts.

Caroline, a president at a public university, echoed the sentiments of Goodall (2009) and Tuchman (2009).

> *People who say they want to be university president when they're young, like when they're assistant professor or professor, I think there's something wrong with them [laughs]. You know, well they shouldn't be research university presidents because you should have much more of a scholarly record because you can't be the president of a research university unless you've walked the walk. You can't tell people to be more productive and publish in better places unless you've done it. So, I think I'm pretty typical like that. But, for different types of institutions, like for example, small liberal arts colleges or non-research universities, sometimes*

> *people didn't come from the tenured faculty. So, they are different kinds of people for different reasons. And then, there are some really weird cases like the University of California system, which has always had a scholar. They made Janet Napolitano [a lawyer and the former United States Secretary of Homeland Secretary] their president. I don't get that at all. I mean, I just don't believe in that. But, so there are weird cases like that. Oh, let's get someone from high up government or industry; that's like me going to run American Airlines – not knowing anything about the business.*

Similarly, Stanley, a dean at a public university that highly values faculty research, offered the following advice to future administrators:

> *Do a lot of really good research and be willing to step forward and do tasks that need to be done. You demonstrate your ability by success and you can't have success if you don't do anything.*

Cynthia, a dean at a private liberal arts college, gave advice to potential administrators who paralleled Caroline and Stanley's insights. She also spoke of the need to have established a pathway that entails spending time in the positions that one will eventually supervise.

> *Well, on the academic side, I would say, it's important to be a great scholar. You know if you want those kinds of positions, you do need to have stood in the shoes of the people, particularly the faculty. So, finishing a dissertation and getting tenure and teaching classes, and it is hard to work with your department heads and the kinds of stuff they have to deal with.*

While my respondents did not all agree that having an esteemed academic portfolio was a necessity for serving in academic leadership roles, most did agree that while there is not a clear pathway that a leader must always follow, a leader must clearly understand and empathize with subordinates' challenges. As such, serving in these roles infers an established academic track record. Making the leap from department head to dean, for example, implies that the leader has a terminal degree and has most likely demonstrated disciplinary expertise. Oftentimes, deans have served as department heads, provosts have served as deans, and presidents have served in senior vice president, provost or deanship roles. Cynthia, a dean at a private liberal arts college, stated:

Being a department head is one of the hardest jobs on the planet. You can't help them with that unless you kind of know what that feels like.

Sabrina, the president at a public university that places a considerable emphasis on faculty teaching and research, addressed the importance of not skipping around through the leadership hierarchy.

Do the jobs that you will supervise. In other words, I was a faculty member, I was a dean, and I was an academic vice president because when you get to the top, you understand the complexity of those jobs. Don't try to skip around and be president and take shortcuts because even though sometimes you say why do I have to do this job, that job, when you get to the top and you're talking to people who are doing the job and you've done it, you are very helpful to them. One: because you understand how hard it is and two: because you can give them insights about your own experience. So, I would say

> *to someone, make sure you do those jobs well as you go along and if it doesn't go well, find out why it didn't go well. But, make sure you're systematic about the way you get to a presidency because in the long run, the people who are most successful are people that understand organizational structures.*

Louis, the provost at a public university that emphasizes faculty teaching and research, also agreed that a properly structured pathway that allows for growth in a variety of academic roles is essential.

> *Yeah, so you get a position as a tenure track faculty member, you get tenure six years later presumably, you can start looking at department administration positions which are always good training ground for academic administration from chair you could go to dean after that.*

Isabella, a provost at a public research university, emphasized the need for scholarship, aspiration, and experience through the ranks of learning other academic positions along the way to a chief leadership role.

> *You know if you have this kind of aspiration. I do think there's a selection bias. You'll find your way there because it's attractive to you. But, having the credibility under your belt, being of good scholarship, having gone through that. I mean, sure we bring people in, I could have come into this job – what qualifies me for this job is really training that I've had in other parts of my career more than anything. But, I wouldn't be credible in this job without having been every single rank and gone through the process and earned all of that because*

> *I was a faculty member for twelve years. And so, I get it. And, I was there. So, there's something powerful just about having been there. As smart and talented as you might be and able to do the job, there is something to putting your time in and so it will give you a lot of credibility and job security.*

My interview with Isabella then shifted to a discussion of credentials and the position. Isabella reasoned her hesitation at the phenomenon of non-Ph.Ds. taking on academic leadership roles.

> *It's a little disconcerting and there is something troubling about academic leadership without really understanding what the core training for that is. So, sometimes I think we hold that in much too much esteem. Sometimes I think we should knock it off; it's just elitist and arrogant. But, sometimes I think, to some extent, there's a real genuine core of what scholarship is that you cannot understand unless you've pursued a Ph.D.*

While it is important for academic leaders to have pursued a Ph.D. and to understand the dedication that is necessary as part of the publication process, some leaders also expressed the importance of understanding the faculty perspective through classroom experience. Administrators emphasized the importance of teaching as a way of staying close to the student and faculty experience given the distractions and possibilities emerging from new technology as well as a changing student body.[2] Ronald, the president of a public university, stated:

> *So, sometimes you wear your academic hat. If you choose to and I often – I say often – maybe, I*

> *haven't done it for maybe a year or two but I used to at least once a year. And, I probably will again – teach a class – a class that I can teach one night a week. So, sometimes I get back into teaching.*

Bradford, a dean at a private university, spoke of his decision to return to the classroom to get a sense of what the faculty members are confronting in their daily encounters with students.

> *I taught last spring. […] And I did that partly for "street creds," cause the faculty would say to me – "you don't know, you haven't taught for X amount of years." So, I said, "fine, I'll teach." And, I had a great experience.*

Bradford shows that he is flexible to other opportunities as they may arise and has not solely pledged to wear an "administrator hat." Faculty members notice this and respect him for this commitment.

Other respondents saw potential for changes in the leadership pathway. Laura, the president of a private liberal arts college, was not convinced that, particularly in the coming years, a Ph.D. and academic credentials were essential for academic administrators. When I asked her about advice for future college presidents, Laura stated:

> *Well, there would be a lot. If you want to be a college president, if that's really a career goal and again I think that's pretty unusual. […] You have to have a passion for the academic side. We have way more presidents now who are coming into these roles after having been a chief development officer or a CFO and I think that's fine. But, I think there is real danger in ascending to one of these roles, leading an institution of higher education if*

you don't really have your heart in the academic experience.

Laura is responding to the "de-churching of higher education." According to Tuchman (2009, p. 41):

higher education is one of the last revered Western institutions to be "de-churched"; that is, it is one of the last to have its ideological justification recast in terms of corporatization and commodification and to become subject to serious state surveillance.

As such, we are seeing the diminution of a reverence for spirited intellectual growth on college campuses that encourages freethinking and creativity, especially among students. The bottom line is often the dollar, and this means that there are spaces for non-Ph.D. or non-traditional academic leaders to ascend to academic leadership roles such as president, in particular. Presidents of universities, while they oversee the operations of the university that encompass the student experience, are also accountable for fundraising and corporate and governmental contracts. Traditional presidents who focused their pre-administration careers on research outside of the applied domains of business, education, government, or leadership, for example, then must really learn on the job. Nadine, the president at a private liberal arts college, also attested to the changing dynamic of the ascendancy to president given that the presidency encompasses so many skills that are not necessarily specific to rigorous academic training:

Right now, if one wanted to be a president, there are multiple career paths that are open. And, so maybe 10 or 15 years ago you really would need to stay a traditional academic route of kind of what I did and I don't think that advice is good

> *anymore because I think there's a greater openness to diversity of paths and frankly diversity of people going into the presidency.*

Christopher, the president of a private university, also spoke of the changing landscape for academic leaders. Yet, Christopher differed from my other interview participants because he earned his Ph.D. later in life when he wanted to (in his words), "burnish [his] credentials to become an administrator." As an MBA graduate, he had an early career in business and served in senior administrative roles at other universities. Christopher spoke about the increasing unattractiveness of the job of university president given this context of the "de-churched university."

> *Regarding higher education in particular, I think the demands of the job of university president in the coming years are going to make it less and less appealing to individuals. And, that's not just my opinion; it's the opinion of most provosts, as you know; that was the traditional track to the college presidency was to first serve as a chief academic officer and then become a provost. All the data suggests that – an increasing number of provosts don't want any part of the job of president because of all the external demands of the job in dealing with the donors and dealing with the government and dealing with all the different constituencies in the neighborhoods when you want to build a building and all those issues I think are a different skillset from those that traditionally have risen through the ranks of academia to become university presidents.*

Given the complexity of this changing landscape, there is limited time for academic administrators to continue their own research. Many of my respondents spoke about being comfortable with having their research take a back seat when they were asked to take on lead roles as deans. Individuals generally become academics because they want to advance their disciplines, not because they have aspirations of ascending to a university presidency. Stella, the president of a private university, spoke of the difficulty that she faced in making the decision to leave her stimulating research behind for administrative work:

> *It was a hard decision because I had my research going at the highest level ever. I had the largest group of graduate students, the most grants. I was enjoying the work at [my past university], immensely. And, all those decisions – it always seems like it will be better in five years. Oh, five years from now, that will be a great thing to do. And, I thought, well, I'm sitting here today and that opportunity isn't here five years from now. It's here today. [...] And, it took a lot of soul searching. I talked to some friends and colleagues of my husband and people I knew in leadership positions. And, I thought a lot about what I was getting gratification from doing all this work for [a project], not just my own research. And so, [a current university president at another institution who had ties to the hiring university] flew out to try to recruit me for the job, and he said, well, think of how many more Ph.D. students you'll have in your career and if you had half as many, but were able to do other things with other people and for other people, – how would you feel about that? And, so he got me to think about the roles in terms of being broader than just my own research and educational work.*

The choice to leave behind world-renowned research projects is clearly a difficult one that Stella confronted in the midst of her burgeoning scholarly career. With the changing demands of university leadership as a result of the de-churching of the university, it is likely that we are going to witness more change that may lead to fewer difficult decisions among faculty members to leave research projects behind if there is a wider acceptance for non-traditional, non-academic university leaders. Christopher stated:

> *I think the profile of the individual college president is going to change. Maybe I'm an example of it because the board here at [my current university] saw in my mix of experiences I think the kind of experience that would be valuable to the challenges that we face in the future. I'd like to think that anyway. But, that doesn't diminish the respect that the president needs to have for the academic side of the house. The recognition of what constitutes quality in an educational institution. You can't not have that; it just I think is getting increasingly important or increasingly possible that you don't have to demonstrate that simply by being a traditional Ph.D., serving as a faculty member, obtaining tenure, becoming a department chair, then a dean, then a provost, then a president. I think you can demonstrate that you appreciate and understand the importance of that academic quality without having done that. If you can do that and bring other skills to the table, now I think you've got a really interesting potential university president.*

While change certainly is upon us, Sophia, a provost at a private university, expressed challenges that she senses as a result of her rising through the ranks of administration without first holding a faculty appointment. Sophia has her Ph.D. and has limited teaching experience. However, she was not certain that she wanted to continue her research when it was time for her to go on the job market. Sophia recognizes the benefits of a more systematic pathway to academic leadership and offered the following piece of advice:

> *The path that I took was really happenstance. There weren't faculty positions that were really open to me at the time and I wasn't sure that that's what I wanted to do. But, if you want to go into academic administration leadership, starting on the tenure track is the way to have full citizenship. Because, not having the faculty side of it is taking a leg off the table.*

Earning citizenship as a leader is key. Leaders can earn their citizenship through publishing path-breaking research, a firsthand understanding of the current student population, and by selflessly demonstrating a deep commitment and sincere care for university needs.

LEADING WITH A STRONG EGO, NOT A BIG EGO

Cultural Respect

Listening to the multiple stakeholder audiences of a university that include students, faculty, staff members, alumni, the Board of Trustees, the community, and corporate and governmental partners gives a leader a sense of the issues that are of key importance. That is not to say that a leader cannot bring in new, transformational ideas; however, it is key, and this came through in my interviews, for a university leader to understand the culture and university values, especially before making any brash decisions (Budig, 2002). As a leader steps into a new role, if not careful, that leader can easily agitate entire constituencies. Ideas and processes from previous institutions do not necessarily transfer well to new contexts.

Samuel, a dean at a private liberal arts college, underscored the importance of respecting an institution's culture and not attempting to change that culture.

> *Well, okay so one thing is we have a pretty clear sense of what the culture of this place is and people want a leader who is able to understand that culture, respect that culture, and not think that the culture needs to be changed completely. Everyone's going to change things a little bit, but the underlying culture of this place should stay the same.*

Similarly, Rachel, the provost at a public university, acknowledged the significance of understanding and preempting faculty responses to change.

> *In order to be successful, one had to acquire an in-depth understanding of those cultural changes otherwise I think whatever any leader attempted to do would not be very successful. That was really critical. Now, I knew that culture was important because I watched the dean who was very successful. But, I watched his successor go up in flames individually, the one with whom I had worked with as associate dean. And, that's simply because he tried to make change, significant change without understanding how the faculty would respond and without understanding the actual culture where he worked. I think I had a conversation with him and I said to him, [name of dean], you know, I think you better pull back*

> *and try to talk to the faculty and understand how they perceive what you're suggesting. I love transformation and am very much in support of meaningful change, but equally as importantly is understanding how one induces change.*

Understanding the proper channels for initiating change is key to the academic leader's operation. Frederick, the president of a private university, upon his arrival noticed a campus culture at his new university where students are particularly vocal in administrative affairs. Frederick approached this freedom of expression and democratic engagement through virtually opening up his office to students through social media. He monitored the campus climate via Facebook, Twitter, and LinkedIn.

Frederick discussed one situation that involved religion, politics and campus organizations. In this instance, a religious group had indicated that individuals who are gay or individuals who were sexually active whether they identified as lesbian, gay, or heterosexual, could not run for organizational leadership positions. The group decided that support for lesbians and gays and sexual activity did not align with their doctrine. Citing how the policy went against the institution's non-discrimination policy, Frederick noted how the committee for student life, comprising students and faculty, addressed the matter finding that leaders should have to adhere to the religious group's guidelines, but that members should be exempt from this parameter. Frederick balanced his personal views with the culture of university deliberation on this incredibly polemic issue:

> *So, we thought that [the committee's decision] was a thoughtful way through this problem but of course all the gay students on campus hated it. They formed a group that petitioned and then they*

> started personally attacking me because I said that
> I thought that the student life committee had made
> a thoughtful and unanimous decision and I would
> support that. But, didn't want to reveal my personal
> preference because my personal preference is we
> should adhere to the non-discrimination policy. So,
> there was a backlash about that and then I tried to
> get out in front of it by talking to them and saying
> to them, look, "I have my own personal views, but
> I think on something like this, we as a community
> have to decide what's the best way forward for us."
> Because, we have two polar views, we tried to come
> up with a compromise. If we feel as a community
> that compromise isn't right, we need to have further
> discussions, further panel discussions and forums
> next semester and see if the committee on student
> life wants to reevaluate it now that they hear
> different opinions. So, that's where we're taking it
> now. But, you know, it's upon that criticism making
> sure you get back out and explain your position
> and why you think you shouldn't decide but the
> community needs to decide for itself because
> there's too often this every time there's a bad thing
> that happens, they expect me to make some great
> pronouncement against it. And, you also can't do
> that for freedom of expression issues.

Clearly, Frederick respects university culture. While he expressed to me that he profoundly disagreed with the group's exclusionary practices, he chose not to intervene further at the risk of rendering the university process meaningless.

While institutional culture is incredibly important for an academic leader to understand and respect, it is also possible for leaders to incite cultural changes. Yet, Stella, the president of a private university, cautions that cultural changes do take time and require broad acceptance from stakeholders. While respondents stressed that it is important to have a deep respect for institutional culture, they also acknowledged the need for leaders to have a vision for change that must not trump the overall institutional culture. Furthermore, that vision or mission does not need to be clearly articulated in a motto-like statement that encapsulates a leader's tenure. Laura, the president at a private liberal arts college, expressed her frustration when the Board Chair of the Board of Trustees asked her "what is your mission?"

> *He kept pushing me on what's my legacy here at [this college] and [...] it occurred to me [...] it's not about my legacy it's about the legacy of our students. It's about the impact that they're going to have. It's not about me. [...] But, I think in terms of leadership style [...] effective leaders are able to set aside their own need for ego strokes. To be able to put that aside and think about what's best for the organization.*

Laura indicated that carrying out her mission meant doing what was most in line with the time-honored college traditions.

> *Well, we have a mission. And, my legacy is to see that mission continue to be supported in a really strong way in a swirling environment. That's the legacy, really. It's thinking and of course you had to think a little differently about that mission today with distance education and all the cost value discussions. Of course, it's very expensive, a residential liberal arts education. But our mission is still so relevant and in terms of legacy I'm really*

> *just thinking about how do we propel that mission forward in a challenging environment. But, I don't see that as a [she inserts her full name here] legacy. It's not like we're taking a brand-new direction here.*

A leader's mission needs to be in the form of enduring attention to the long-term institutional benefit, and not as a catchy legacy statement. The leader is a vehicle for initiating institutional change; it is not the leader who will go down in institutional history. Rather, the value of what the leader originates leaves an indelible mark on the university.

CARING FOR THE INSTITUTION

Effective academic leaders put the needs of the institution above their own personal careers. Perceptions that a leader is merely making a brief stop at this particular institution to appeal to a more prestigious institution, that the leader does not respect the position and its larger meaning to the university community, or that a leader cannot adequately deal with personnel matters, are all manifestations of ineffective leadership.

While it is likely that academic leaders will move around, faculty, in particular, often disparage the "career academic" who sees the university position that they presently occupy as a stepping-stone to the next opportunity. Tuchman (2009, p. 70) writes about this phenomenon: "the possibility of satisfying ambition is not a sufficient reason to take a job at Wannabe University." While professional development and movement for new challenges, greater opportunities, and increased pay are certainly lauded within corporate and governmental contexts, higher education administration operates a bit differently.

Many of my respondents cautioned against self-promotion, characterized by a dismissal of institutional values, at the cost of moving the institution in a direction that would gain them individual external prestige and recruiter attention.

Matthew, the dean of a private university, spoke in-depth about his own lack of interest in ever ascending to a leadership position. However, he found himself being recommended for department chair that subsequently led to his deanship. Matthew addressed his views toward careerism and the academic presidency:

> *So, I think that my sense is that in academic administration, generally there's a lot of work around the last fifteen years where administrations try to find ways not to go through the main faculty organs because they don't do what they want or they're too slow. And I have some negative views of why that's happening and it's probably because of careerism among presidents so the people are thinking of a five-year career impact and they can't wait for us to percolate and then to say that we didn't like it after all which is what we've been doing lately; mowing things down after people put in tons of work.*

At Matthew's university, he has personally witnessed the unconstructive consequences of having presidents in office whose missions do not match institutional values. When those presidents leave, those who are left behind end up modifying the careerist president's unsympathetic decisions.

Laura, the president at a private liberal arts college, expressed how her non-careerist ambitions as a college administrator might have led to her attractiveness for the position among the presidential search committee at her institution. Many perceived her unsuccessful predecessor who had a very short tenure as president, to be on a career track. Laura stated:

> *I think the reason that people wanted me in this role was a response to her leadership which was much less, certainly less passionate about the institution. I think there were perceptions that maybe she was kind of on a career track and didn't really care so much about [name of the college] and really never quite understood it so well. And so, [I] began to shape what I saw was really important which was to return the focus to our mission and our students and what's important.*

Laura was perfectly content as a faculty member and enjoyed teaching and publishing. She, much like the majority of my respondents, was not particularly interested in leadership during her early career. Mentoring and support from others prompted Laura and others to consider leadership roles. Yet, that is not to say that careerist ambitions cannot form once a leader has a taste for the job. Careerist agendas are more likely to be found among leaders who are external to an institution given that leaders may be moving around as new opportunities arise and they learn from them through headhunters' recruitment efforts (Tuchman, 2009). I do not wish to paint the picture that leaders with intentional leadership or careerist agendas are not capable of respecting and valuing what is best for the institution. Presidents and provosts, in particular, are often placed as a result of external searches and deeply care about the future of the institutions where they are leading. On the other hand, careerist agendas entail a lack of care for the institution in favor of a leader's own professional gain. Being a career-minded university leader with prospects for moving to another institution does not necessarily mean one is an ineffective leader, but eschewing a careerist persona is an important asset.

HAIL TO THE POSITION

Successful leaders also demonstrate respect for their position, their predecessors and future successors, and what their current position means to the institution. Denise, the president at a private liberal arts college, spoke about the importance of honoring institutional traditions that are a part of institutional culture. Denise addressed how she observed the actions of two presidents that she had served under in a previous institution. She compared each of these presidents' relationships to their presidential roles:

And, in comparing them to each other, obviously, I can't hope to have the best of both, but I can see what I admired about each of them and I felt that the first president was a particularly good communicator and very good at understanding his role in the community, so he was a little bit, he might strike you when you saw him up close, working with him he was a little bit maybe pretentious in a sense like you felt that he was kind of full of the role. But, when you look at it from the outside, you see how important that is that he came across really wonderfully in all public occasions; he knew the right thing to say. [Name of other president], the president I worked with most recently, is much better to work with as a kind of person and in terms of how he listens. But, he wasn't as good initially at kind of presenting himself because he just wasn't that into the role. [...] But, he just wouldn't take the role as seriously. He was kind of impatient with the ceremony and so he would say people don't really want me to talk here. Let's just skip the remarks. And, that feels like a kind of humility, but then people would be

> *disappointed. And so, one of the things that I really learned from that is that if you're the president it's not about you and your ego, it's about the role and that in some sense, inhabiting the role properly means taking it seriously.*

Depending on the size of a campus community, some members of the community may only have a handful of occasions when they may come into contact with the president, provosts, or deans. If a leader disparages the meaning of their official remarks, it can be seen as disrespectful. Denise indicates that the leader must realize that a leadership role must not be egocentric; the effective leader must assume all of the components of the job with veneration for the institutional history.

> *And, even in my time so far at [my present institution], I've had to really come to grips with that. That here, I'm treated as important. I'm almost a celebrity in town; people recognize me and they come up to me and they introduce themselves and say, "oh, you're the new president." And, it's hard at first not to feel like you want to resist that because it feels kind of self-inflating. But, when you recognize it's not about you because they don't even know you yet, it's about the role and the fact that the president of [name of college] is an important person in this town and in this community. Then you have to learn to be more gracious about it and instead of feeling flustered or hesitant about it, sort of feel like that's part of my job is to take seriously the idea that I'm important to these people and that they notice if I show up at something and if I stop and chat with someone in the grocery store, then*

> *later I hear; "oh, so and so was so pleased that you spoke to them." It's kind of funny at first, but when you take it seriously; you realize that it means that the ego part of it has to be about the role and not about you. And, I would say that that's something that in looking at the two presidents I work with, one was much better at than the other. And, I think [name of president] became much better at it over time. But, it was never natural to him. I think he just didn't like the ceremonial aspects of things. And, I actually – I like those things and I think that the trick will be to not get an inflated ego about it because you don't want to feel like it's about you. But, in some sense recognizing that part of what the institution wants is that kind of symbolic head where you coming to something and talking to people signifies it's an important event and that means that you are in that context important.*

Denise quickly understood the importance of respecting the office and leaving her own ego aside for the goodness of the institution. Paul, a president at a private liberal arts college, spoke about ego-related issues pertaining to his presidential predecessor and his realization that a leader ought to prioritize the needs of the institution's stakeholders.

> *But, I think those people who are most successful in these jobs tend to have certain characteristics generally and they're not found more widely in the public as I said they're assiduous learners, they're really interested in every time they sit down with someone in their meeting, they want to know what the issue is. They want to understand it; they're fascinated by all of the things that go into creating*

> *these kinds of institutions. They're good listeners
> [...] they're good communicators.*

Being a good listener means intentional listening. An effective leader listens to understand and to facilitate options for the communicator. Paul then connected his thoughts on listening and caring for others' insights to the concept of an egotistical leader who is so self-absorbed and falls short of properly stewarding university interests. Paul continued:

> *But, beyond that, I think someone once said this to me and I think it's really quite right. It's very important to have a strong ego in this job but not so good to have a big ego and there's a big difference. There are lots of people in these jobs who get caught up in being the president. They think they're funnier than they are, they think they're more entertaining than they are because everybody always laughs at them even though they – they lose sight of who they are. That's a big mistake and these jobs can be humbling and they should be humbling. But to have a strong ego is to believe that you're qualified to do this job, you have confidence in your own abilities. And, that your own capacity to help create change in a positive institution, while also being capable of as I said before of listening.*

Paul's encounter with his predecessor who was an extraordinarily poor listener with a big ego helped him to illustrate leadership downfalls and the poor mentoring and advice that he received from his predecessor and ended up ignoring.

Leaders with big egos are excessively proud of their accomplishments and have exorbitant self-esteem marked by their perception that they are somehow better than those who they are leading. On the other hand, leaders with strong egos know that they are the right person for the job and do not need to have their egos stroked by anyone. They get the facts by doing their own research and by talking to relevant stakeholders. Leaders with strong egos respect their position and its vital importance to the institution. They are not looking for self-promotion; rather, they respect their position to such an extent that they understand their personal importance to the university community. Respondents also noted the importance of leaving one's ego at the door and establishing a community-driven agenda instead of a personally driven agenda.

PERSONNEL ISSUES

Being able to separate personal matters from work-related matters plays a key role in a leader's ability to handle personnel issues. Many of my respondents addressed the stressful circumstances of having to communicate an unsuccessful tenure application, asking a department chair to step down given a hostile department situation, firing a faculty or staff member, or simply calming the waters in a controversial staff-related situation.

Eugene, a dean at a public university who had an open office door policy that opened himself up to both praise and criticism, noted the solid advice that he received from a mentor regarding how to deal with individuals' disagreements with leadership decisions. Eugene recalled that his mentor stated:

> *There will be days that people may even insult you, that people may disagree with you and there will be days when people come and praise you. Do not take any of those two seriously, okay? Keep your*

eye on the ball and also have a very very weak short memory about bad experiences. I would say that if somebody comes in here and insulted me and did everything. The minute the person leaves this room; I try to forget about it. I've had situations where people hung up the phone at me and that person expected me to react – you know, maybe not talk to the person or don't acknowledge them when I see. I did exactly the opposite. The first chance I got to see this person, I walked in, I greeted the person, I shook hand and I said – how are you?

Many of my respondents commented that personnel issues were the most difficult to tackle. Anna, a provost at a public university, talked about the sensitive and time-consuming nature of making personnel changes:

Last year though we integrated the entire [name of center] so I moved 78 people and they had tried to do it two other times before and we just did it. In the course of a year, we moved 78 positions from across the street over to here. We integrated two instructional design units. We integrated people into the Registrar's, into the Bursar's office. We integrated faculty so to move 78 people – to close down a unit and reinvent it here – extremely challenging and I had to meet with the union, I had to meet with HR multiple times. I had to meet with individuals. I had to sit across from people who were crying and telling me – they all kept their jobs but it was a unit that had not been very effective. It was running in the hole and we integrated all of that across the street. It's done. Everybody's fine.

On a more drastic note, Samuel, a dean at a private liberal arts college, spoke in-depth about a situation in which he had to fire a faculty member who had a positive, established institutional working history:

I had been in this office for less than a year and I got an email from someone I had never met before. I don't know the name, saying how can you have appointed so and so as chair of the department? She doesn't even have a Bachelor's degree. Okay, this is a woman who by the way – the faculty member in question was the senior most Asian woman on campus, had tenure from [her previous institution] where we hired her away, chair of the department for the last 13 years, she had been here for 14 years so it was 14 years that she was chair because we brought her in as chair. So, she was a really senior person. So, I considered this kind of a nuisance letter. So, I said to my assistant at the time, okay, I want to be able to – I don't want to let this sit cause these are the kinds of things that can get really nasty. So, call [the university where she obtained her Bachelor's degree], get ahold of the verifications desk, get a copy, have them send us a copy of her transcript and then I'll write back and I can tell this person that everything's okay and that's why. So, I came back from lunch and my assistant's hand was like shaking. And, I said, what's the matter [name of assistant]? And, she said, well the letter is right. She doesn't have even a Bachelor's degree. [...] Well, they didn't check 14 years ago. And, they didn't check at [name of university] where she had been a tenured professor. So, that was a big challenge because we were just, I had just announced this

> *major initiative around diversifying our faculty and I'm going to take our senior Asian woman and fire her. And, you'd be surprised that some of our faculty after this happened actually wrote to the local newspaper, decrying me for firing her.*

Samuel continued this discussion by commenting on this process and his role in ensuring that this fraudulently tenured professor would not continue to be a part of his institution.

> *I've told that story before, but I would say something about it, which is that although it's really hard at moments like that. It isn't difficult to know what you're supposed to do.*

In carrying out an unpleasant task of dismissing a member of the college or university community, a leader needs to reflect on the importance of the decision to the institution's future. Samuel realized the meaning and optics of firing an esteemed faculty member who happened to be from a historically marginalized population; however, he understood how the significance of this dismissal was not about race, it was about the future respect of the institution as an influential liberal arts college. Samuel and many of my respondents spoke about the need for leaders to value a diversity of opinions that among my participants, centered on matters pertaining to race, gender, or disciplinary origin.

VALUING DIVERSITY OF OPINIONS

Education and leadership scholars confirm the importance of administrators demonstrating a respect for diversity among the students, faculty, and community at large (Bowen & Bok, 2000; Bruch, Jehangir, Lundell, Higbee, & Miksch, 2005;

Tuchman, 2009). My respondents were exceptionally aware of the need for a university-wide respect for a diversity of opinions.

Frederick, a president at a private university, spoke about his experience in fielding concerns from young women students who had been raped. I asked Frederick if he held open office hours and he talked about this as a future possibility because of what it meant about obtaining a variety of views on key issues:

No, I don't. It's something I might want to do next year. My provost has done it and has had great success. I just have it, as any student who wants to invite me to lunch, wants to come see me, they can do that. But, maybe what I've noticed with [the provost's name] and the way he's having office hours. He gets a group dynamic going. So, they actually come because they have different issues, but then you get the perspective of the other people who are there who didn't actually come to talk about that issue, and so the group dynamic is interesting [...] especially, if you get students, and faculty, and staff in the group at the same time.

Frederick then continued to talk about how students established rapport with him via Facebook and how that led to their openness and frankness during in-person meetings.

Women who have been raped, recently in the past month, I've had two women come see me about being raped or problems with alcohol. Things that – and it's interesting how they used Facebook to build up the trust to come see me. It wasn't "Hi President [Frederick's last name], can I come see you about my personal matter? It was a series of

> *communications by messaging that they built up the trust with me that they could then come and see me. And, you wouldn't get that by email, it's too formal.*

This example demonstrates two facets of valuing a diversity of opinions. Frederick addressed how through open in-person dialogues, a diversity of ideas can be shared and discussed. Furthermore, these dialogues allow individuals from unaffected constituencies to weigh in on more global university matters. In addition, Frederick demonstrated how his openness through social media established a sense of trust between him and the students. College women victims, who had recently experienced rape, felt comfortable enough to come to Frederick to talk to him about matters that the university could institute to protect students. I asked if the college women who were rape victims had suggestions for him and he stated:

> *Yes, and we have a 12-page document from a group who wanted us to – they realized that we have done a lot with our sexual assault policy, it's much better than it was. We actually were ahead of the game before any of this happened; before all the stuff blew up at [another major university] we were well ahead with a better policy, with a better way to deal with it. They would like more and they have certain issues about certain things. So, it's just improvements and we've agreed to have a working group that would include them and the staff and maybe a faculty member to get it better and we're happy to do that. It's going to require more resources, but I think they're pleased that we're engaging them in the process.*

Frederick demonstrated his willingness to talk to diverse constituents whose interests and viewpoints were of key importance to him. He realized that establishing a framework for how to move forward with regard to dealing with rape on his campus would require campus buy-in from the students, staff, and faculty members.

Before arriving on campus, via social media, Frederick made it a point of connecting with as many of the university professionals at his incoming university as possible. He did not live close to his incoming university and took advantage of LinkedIn's services. He reported:

> *So, I had joined LinkedIn for professional reasons. [...] And, then I realized it was a wonderful way for me to introduce myself to the community. So, I started ten a day connecting with [name of university] administrative staff, saying "Hi, I'm the new president, I'd like to connect with you." Then, if they connected with me, I'd say, "tell me a little bit about what you do at the university and what you think I need to know as the new president." And, I'd get success rates of connections, probably 90% because they were curious. And, by the time I had arrived here, I had about 1200 connections with [name of university] people each of which had written two or three paragraphs to me about what their job was, who they were, how long they'd been here, their warm wishes to me as the new president and what they thought I needed to know.*

Firsthand meetings and social media connections launched a mechanism for Frederick to pay attention to the diverse demands and needs of the university. He invited all members of the university to engage him in dialogue.

Paul, a president at a private liberal arts college, spoke of his respect for students' disregard for a building on campus, dedicated to the study of civil rights, that had a racially insensitive plaque and did not acknowledge the civil rights achievements of people of color with only paintings and acknowledgements of white people throughout the building. Paul described the situation and how he resolved to modify this existing structure that had been a college landmark and that bore the name of a prominent funding family.

> *There was no reference whatsoever given in the building to civil rights, as we understand them. No Martin Luther King, no nothing. And, [...] there was a plaque put on the wall inside the building that talked about the right of Anglo Saxons to own property and students and many people in the community saw the language of it all as being perhaps racist because it talked about civil rights in the eyes of the people who built this structure.*

Paul was exceptionally driven to deal with this situation given that for years, Paul's predecessors had not addressed this glaring issue.

> *When I arrived in [year], the building hadn't changed one bit. And there was this very strong deeply held view that the building was out of touch with the community. And the people were very resentful about it. Students were resentful, faculty were resentful. They believed that nothing could be done about it because in part, my predecessor and others told them nothing could be done about it. The donors, who are still involved in the college, wouldn't want that to be dealt with. Over the years, petitions have been raised about how this building*

> *is racist and its various protests were discussed about why the hell do we have a building on civil rights that has nothing to do with civil rights, as we understand it today.*

Paul chose to engage the community in an open dialogue about the fate of this building. What follows is Paul's account of how this controversial situation turned into a teachable moment:

> *Who built this structure? What was civil rights supposed to be [so many decades ago]? How did people understand what it was and why is it that the building has never evolved? So, we went through a whole process and to make a long story a little shorter, that task force came up with a series of recommendations. I engaged the family that were the donors for this and I told them respectfully what we were doing and I told them I'm sure you're interested in this too that this is the issue. They were completely supportive. There was no issue for them. The students were making some demands that were unreasonable like to tear the plaque down and various things and instead I suggested why don't we make a new plaque. […] Let's create a new plaque that explains civil rights today and that shows this was civil rights [then] and this is civil rights [now] We created an art exhibition on the history of civil rights at [name of college] and in the world that is in the lobby of that building so that now there are all kinds of faces, not just white men with historical contexts explaining the evolution of civil rights as an idea and then finally we had a dedication ceremony […].*

Paul, who noted the importance of "checking your ego at the door" in this situation, was able to bring a variety of individuals including historical figures, the funding family, and the student and faculty community, into the same room to celebrate the meaning of civil rights today and to eliminate the 80-year polemic divide inherent in this building's messaging. Paul's strong ego, not his big ego, guided his decisions in the above situation. He did what was best for the campus community by paying attention to diversity, in the sense of racial diversity and inclusion. In addition, he valued diversity with regard to whose opinions mattered to the college; he did not hesitate to enlist support from the wealthy donor family as his predecessor had.

Similarly, Ronald, the president of a public university, talked about the need for an effective leader to be able to take a wide variety of diverse views and find ways of channeling them into a new direction. Ronald summed up a key point about the role of an effective leader with regard to differences of opinion:

> *Well, I think effective leadership in higher education is being able to take a wide variety of very diverse, divergent, not sometimes fairly acrimonious and strongly held positions and find reasons for all of these different, or the majority of these different groups and thoughts to find a place inside of a new direction.*

Lastly, Bradford, a dean at a private university, and Rachel, a provost at a public university, addressed the importance of respect for disciplinary diversity. As such, a chemist may approach a problem differently than a sociologist would because of different training in problem solving. I asked Bradford to consider a quality that is important for an aspiring leader to embody. He stated:

Breadth of understanding and I've said this and by that, I mean beyond your discipline. I have to understand, I don't have to understand chemistry, but I have to understand chemists. Early on when I was an associate dean we had a committee meeting and we decided that the faculty would read Benjamin Franklin's autobiography, now that's a literary choice. And we all read it and we met at the beginning of school and had this great faculty meeting and lunch. And, one of the chemists said, all summer long he would do this to me. He would say, Bradford, today Benjamin Franklin went swimming. What's the point? Today, he ate the bread and got laughed at, Bradford what's the point? Bradford, I'm reading a story, why am I reading a story? And, I would say because Benjamin Franklin is a quintessential American and everything he does has been saturated into our culture and you can learn tons from him. […] And, you know, for him it wasn't a really successful thing. However, chemists' thinking can be incredibly useful to a college. They are smart; they handle enormous structures that my brain gives up on step B. They can run a curriculum committee; they are problem solvers. One of my associate deans is a chemist and I have to learn as a leader what contribution can this person bring? What is it that sociologists bring what is it that chemists bring, what is it that poets bring? Because as a leader, if you can get that; it's almost like conducting an orchestra. If you can really get that discussion going, there's just no better brain trust in the world than the liberal arts faculty.

Bradford, with literary disciplinary origins, realizes that he approaches problems differently from his peers. Yet, he realizes that through valuing diversity in what each individual brings to the table, a university can function in harmony.

Rachel also acknowledges the importance of disciplinary diversity and discusses how it was crucial for her to come to understand the differences in individuals' work styles that are often rooted in their disciplines. Here, she talks about her experience working as an associate dean of arts and sciences at a much larger university:

> *For the first time, I worked very closely with the science faculty because it was the arts and the sciences which then required that I acquire an understanding of the differences in the disciplines as well as the appreciation of how one discipline either intersects with or complements the other. So, [...] it pulled me out of the social science humanities areas and really in many ways forced me to acquire a more in-depth understanding of interdisciplinarity and then even more importantly, how to communicate across all disciplines. But, while in the role, the fact that I was a woman never played a part. It's all about your skill sets.*

In discussing the effective leadership strategies, Rachel noted how the importance of understanding disciplinary differences trumped gender identity matters. In her new role, Rachel learned that being able to speak across disciplines and to bring people together toward a common vision were of key importance.

Building broadly diverse teams came up in many of my interviews. Martha, a dean at a public university, and Stanley, a dean at a public university, each discussed the importance of team diversity. Stanley cautioned against the unintended consequences of tokenism (Kanter, 1977; Williams, 1989) that might end up disadvantaging historically underrepresented populations including women, openly gay or lesbian individuals, or people of color whose views have not been taken into account in earlier contexts. Stanley noted:

> *Right, they [women of color, in this context] get asked to do everything. It's one of the challenges that leaders face. How do you protect the young faculty from being overused particularly when they have one of those distinctive characteristics, they're the only woman, they're the only minority, whatever it might be. On the one hand, you want diversity in these committees. On the other hand, if you ask them to do that, they never get their research done so they never become an associate or a full professor.*

Stanley acknowledges some of the difficulties associated with teambuilding and committee work. Yet, the respondents were also especially cognizant of the need for establishing solid teams for both current and future work.

TEAMWORK

Collaborative and communal leadership styles are often the most effective leadership styles. Earlier, I noted how women are often more receptive to a collaborative leadership style that involves shared governance and a lack of singly defined decisions (Eagly & Johnson, 1990). Furthermore, I discussed how women often confront a balancing act of managing their communality and their agentic qualities as leaders (Eagly & Carli, 2007; Heilman & Okimoto, 2007). I mention this gendered distinction because scholars have identified a tendency among men to exhibit an agentic approach to leadership

(Eagly & Carli, 2007; Koenig et al., 2011; Spence & Buckner, 2000). Yet, my research denotes just the opposite. Frederick's extraordinary achievements working with rape victims and student groups, Bradford's acknowledgement of disciplinary diversity in group dynamics, and Paul's efforts to work with concerned students, faculty, and donors demonstrate how these men were successfully able to work collaboratively.

Teamwork and shared governance are not just tactics that women leaders employ. Caring about the institution means supporting the work of others to build a contingency of future leaders and sharing the credit. Since one person on a college campus rarely resolves major issues, teamwork is a key component of effective leadership. Douglas, the president of a public university, talked about realizing that his role was about helping others, not self-promotion:

> *I sound like I'm talking right out of a textbook. But, quite frankly, I've found that this is true. I think that the longer I've done this work, the more humble I get. And, I think understanding that you have to make others – you go across this if you have a career in academia, you go across this threshold from where you're happy that I published this great article or I won this teaching award or something to – Boy! I helped Jason or Mary win that teaching award or they got this big grant and that's great for us. It's almost like having children. You kind of go across that and I don't even mean in a paternalistic, you stop thinking about yourself. When I was talking to our graduating top business students I cited one of the last articles that Peter Drucker wrote in* Harvard Business Review *in 2004 when he talked about the importance of pronouns in management and leadership. When you have*

> *to think we and not I and that's what successful*
> *organizations do. And, I think successful leaders do.*

Leadership is about embodying a selfless understanding of the position. As such, leaders need to value each and every constituency as part of a team-based structure.

Marcus, a provost at a public university, provided advice that mirrored much of what Douglas had to say:

> *I think I would tell that person [an aspiring leader] that if they want to be successful, they have to figure out how to be an integral part of a team and to be such an important contributor to that team that everybody else around you wants to follow what you're doing and to always take the extra step or extra two steps beyond what's expected of you so whoever you're reporting to or your manager, if they say, I want you to do such and such area – take that plus an extra one or two things to show that you have that broader capability.*

Marcus addresses collaboration and rising to the occasion when teams could truly benefit. Similarly, Eugene, a dean at a public university, noted:

> *Leaders have to be honest about the fact that leaders are not experts in every field and every area. Leadership requires being able to put a very effective team together and use the talents and the skills and the expertise of everybody […].*

Earlier, I addressed how shared governance and communal leadership styles were an important component of leadership to many of the respondents. In my research, I did not encounter one respondent who felt they could do the job without the support of an effective team.

Teamwork, for some of the respondents, was visible through a sharing of credit and the mentoring and encouragement of future leaders. Joanne, a provost at a private liberal arts college, talked about the importance of nurturing future leaders:

> *I think you also have to think about how you foster the next leader. So, whether it's making sure you're providing good professional development opportunities for your – the administrators that report to you. Or, to the faculty because I think a good leader cares about the institution after she steps down.*

Similarly, Louis, a provost at a public university, spoke about the role that a leader plays in identifying future leaders from the ranks of the faculty and staff:

> *I think that's part of what I try to do is to recognize the potential for leadership through these frequent interactions with colleagues in meetings. Who's showing good judgment, who's listening, who's, it's hard to say exactly what those qualities are. But, you can see them and [...] I would say it's fairly rare.*

Maria, a dean at a public university, spoke about the importance of mentoring junior faculty who could then eventually move into leadership positions. Here, Maria talks about how her institution worked to facilitate a friendly working environment for junior women who were faculty of color:

> *And, a group of our – then almost all – I guess they were all junior women faculty of color – formed a group. [...] And, it was not about – you know – just supporting each other. It was about doing their*

> *work together. And, so they created a structure for sharing their scholarship. They came to me and to the person who was our Associate Vice Provost for Diversity and got money to do a residential two weeks away at a facility that [the university] owns [...] where it was all about writing, sharing their drafts, etcetera. They've done this once every year and it's been a fantastic group. And, I've worked with some of them individually. But, I've also met with them occasionally as a group just to you know navigate the shoals of things. And they are all now – the original group is all now tenured. And, now we've begun to talk about the step from associate to full. And, that's just one example.*

Maria sees her role as a dean as a team-based role. One way that she measures success in her job is by how well the faculty members are advancing.

In line with this understanding of teamwork, Gina, a dean at a public university, noted how she felt that her role was similar to what Maria described above. When I asked Gina to define effective leadership, she stated:

> *How I define it for myself I suppose, is as a leader of a group of people, it's my job to inspire people and to facilitate people to do what they're good at and to accomplish their particular goals. So, I believe that I need to create the space, the proper environment, and the proper atmosphere where people can grow and develop and thrive in their own particular areas.*

Gina felt that she was effectively carrying out her professional mission if she was providing an ideal working community for the faculty, her team members.

Fostering a community of teamwork also means working with staff members to ensure that their views are incorporated into the operations of the institution. Sophia, a provost at a private university, spoke about an instance in which she implemented ideas that three administrative assistants shared with her over lunch. They were frustrated that they did not get advance notice of asbestos removal since they would have likely taken vacation around those days to avoid exposure. Sophia describes her response:

> *And, so what I did is I said, well let's develop listservs so that there can be an automatic e-mail that the physical plant sends out in an office when work's going to be done. Well, it turns out – the physical plant has wanted this for years. But they didn't know how to get it and the administrative assistants have wanted it, but they don't know how to get it. So, you know it's connecting all of the pieces together because in my role, I can do that. [...] Anyway, the point is that once this was done and I sent an announcement out to campus, I thanked the three administrative assistants who had suggested it. And, they were so tickled – they felt like great – because they were given credit as if it was their idea and it was their idea. [...] I wanted them to feel like it's a great idea to tell the associate provost or anybody in the administration that you have an idea and it might actually lead to something that everybody wants.*

Sophia demonstrated her commitment to a team-based environment in which there was credit sharing for new ideas.

Sharing the credit and fostering a sense of collaborative teamwork among a leader's staff members and faculty facilitate successful examples of academic leadership. Placing the importance of the institution above all else and considering the culture, the historical values, the need for objectivity and directness in controversial personnel matters, and considering a diversity of viewpoints in deliberations also demonstrate how a leader can lead with a strong ego, but not a big ego. Effective leaders are transparent and listen and gather the data before implementing policy changes.

NOTES

1. While Goodall (2009) and Tuchman's (2009) research does not specifically address leaders of colleges and universities that are more teaching focused than research focused. This argument can be extended to teaching-focused institutions. As such, the small liberal arts college that focuses on teaching excellence in its mission ought to have a leader at its helm who has demonstrated a balance between teaching and scholarship.

2. Not all of the administrators were capable of remuneration for teaching courses as a result of their union contracts. As such, it makes sense why some administrators would opt not to teach. They would not have been financially compensated for this extra nonessential work on top of all of their other required duties.

3

LEARNING HOW TO BE AN ACADEMIC LEADER

Leaders learn how to lead; they are not born knowing how to lead. Socialization through education (Giroux & Purpel 1983; Jackson, 1990; Margolis & Romero, 1998), peer groups (McFarland & Thomas, 2006), religion (Smidt, 1980), and familial experiences (Buchman & DiPrete, 2006; Thomson & McLanahan, 2012) can motivate an individual's leadership pathway (Al-Lamky, 2007; Suarez-Mccrink, 2002). Socioeconomic status and access to social capital (Mills, 1956; Petev, 2013) can also foster leadership opportunities. How then are academic leaders socialized? What are the processes by which academics decide to pursue leadership positions? What mechanisms prepare leaders for the challenges that lie ahead?

EARLY PATHWAY TO ACADEMIC LEADERSHIP AND MENTORS

Disciplinary passion, devotion for the university experience, and knowledge production are integral components for the burgeoning academic leader (Birnbaum, 1992; Goodall, 2009).

Overall, reverence toward the academic experience is a quality that I observed in each of the 34 interviews. Respondents typically indicated a positive early university experience marked by solid relationships with peers and faculty members that inspired an academic career. Respondents often spoke about a mentor who encouraged research collaboration and their subsequent graduate school matriculation.

There is an abundance of literature on the importance of mentoring. Research addresses its relationship to building campus communities with diverse leadership from historically underrepresented populations (Green & King, 2001; Kezar, Eckel, Contreras-McGavin, & Quaye, 2008), fostering student achievement (Martin & Dowson, 2009; Plucker, 1998), and career success (Scandura & Schriesheim, 1994; Uk Chun, Sosik, & Yun, 2012). Through mentoring, those who are already in positions of influence as professors or administrators identify individuals who possess qualities that indicate a solid potential for professional growth. Furthermore, they may cultivate these individuals by encouraging them to seek challenges. Graduate students often credit their college professors as an integral component to their choice to pursue graduate studies and begin the academic career. Mentoring works on a continuum and is important in all stages of a leader's career.

UNDERGRADUATE AND GRADUATE SCHOOL EXPERIENCE

When I asked my respondents to talk about their path to their particular leadership role, some of them began by discussing their undergraduate experiences. Marcus, a provost at a public university, talked about the significance that mentors played in his early professional growth.

> *Even if it's contentious – it's that one relationship that's going to shape your future and I've been really blessed where I've had three or four mentors along the way that spent the time with me and I'll just share with you briefly that part of the reason why I think I fit so well with this institution is that most of our students – are the first in their family to go to college and that includes me, that I was the first in my family. And, I remember that sort of awkward beginning phase where I had no clue of how to progress from an entry-level university student to graduate school and beyond. All of that was new territory, but I had mentors who – they didn't care about any of that. All they saw was potential I had inside of myself and figured out a way to bring it out of me.*

Given that Marcus was a first-generation college student, the fact that his college professors saw promise in his research potential was especially consequential for his career development.

Joanne, a provost at a private liberal arts college, also talked about how a faculty mentor inspired her to pursue graduate studies.

> *This [being a professor] came as a result of doing research with a particular faculty member who really encouraged me and took me to scientific conferences. So, I started doing research when I was a sophomore in college. And, I would say that that was a very important experience that led me then to go to graduate school [...] I didn't have that as a career goal when I first started college.*

On another note, Christopher, the president of a private university and the only respondent to have achieved his terminal degree while he was already serving in university administration, talked about how his relationship with the president of his undergraduate institution sparked his interest in academic administration.

> *I have a unique path to this job. When I went to [name of university] as an undergrad, I got to know the university president at the time and it was a great privilege to know the university president as a student. And, he was the one who really first created the possibility that working in higher ed would be a really compelling and interesting career. In fact, I say that quite a bit; [name of president] … was the one who had suggested [academic leadership]. In fact, he said in particular that it could be a meaningful, even noble calling.*

On the other hand, Caroline, the president of a public university, talked about her career progression by emphasizing the importance of her graduate school experiences in fostering her decision to pursue an academic leadership position.

> *For graduate school, I had two [mentors]. I had one who was my academic mentor like you probably have and then I had a woman who was an associate dean in my school, in my department who was – she was a mentor to me – like a cheerleader and somebody who was a sounding board. […] So […] those two people were critical. And, then when I was an assistant professor at [name of university] and then I was an associate professor – there was a woman in central administration who's still there – she's Secretary to the Board. […] She really put me on the right committees and got me a lot of experience with central administration. So, I was lucky that*

> *way – fundraising. You know a lot of people don't have somebody like that who's that high up who took an interest in them. So ... I keep in touch with her and every job change I've talked about – I mean I've considered, I talk to her. She didn't always agree with me.*

Regardless of the timing of the mentoring through undergraduate or graduate experiences, mentors' identification of exceptional scholarship and leadership potential made an impression on respondents' pathways. It was through this socialization that respondents came to realize their academic and leadership potential.

FACULTY/ADMINISTRATOR EXPERIENCE

Post tenure, leadership opportunities really open up for professors who are visible on campus, engaged in university governance matters, and who demonstrate openness to the campus community are frequently sought after for leadership positions, at a variety of levels of service. Early on in their academic leadership careers, respondents spoke of being called to serve as department chair as well as to serve the community through participation on university-wide committees. Respondents did not necessarily talk about mentors who guided them toward leadership paths during their years as non-administrative faculty; however, they did focus to a great extent on the importance of mentoring once they took on their first leadership roles. Mentoring came from both within the institution and outside of the institution.

Sabrina, the president of a public university, talked about the importance of a former college president who supported her early career progression when she was a recent Ph.D.

> *He was a college president from whom I worked as a fellow ... while I was in that fellowship program, for that year. He was my mentor. He was very good. He was very supportive, very engaged in the work I was doing. He gave me good feedback. I always got good evaluations. He was constructive in helping me develop my skills.*

Mentoring does not necessarily need to be on a hierarchical level with a mentor in the giving role and the mentee in the receiving role. Maria, a dean at a public university, talked about how once she was in her faculty role, mentorship for her was more about collaborative work than it was about a formal mentoring role. She noted:

> *I was tenured [and] it was more a question of collaborators rather than mentors. The person I mentioned in the geography department – who, we've never been in a situation where she was actually superior to me in some ways but she certainly was someone who had more years at the university and had been there longer than I. And, I continue to use her as an advisor.*

Cynthia, a dean at a private liberal arts college, talked about mentorship from her peers who she also considers to be her friends and solid confidants. When I asked Cynthia to consider who had helped her shape her career as an academic leader, she stated:

> *[Name of woman senior administrator at a previous institution where Cynthia served on the faculty and administration] again I think as a leader, as a leader in higher ed has been an incredible mentor to me. I've had other people who have*

> *been more fleeting...so I think mentors can also be they're not always ahead of you. There are several faculty members at [name of previous institution] who are very close friends of mine but I think we mentor one another. So, [name of woman] in the History Department, [name of woman] in Women and Gender Studies ... those are all people that I admire ..., I admire their smarts and I admire how they think about things. If I need to think through something, they're the people that I go to. I can trust them and I just think they're smart about how to you know, how not to lose your temper. How to be effective to get things done.*

Cynthia's mentors had never performed the exact job that she currently held. Yet, she went to these individuals for support in challenging times.

Mentors can play a crucial role in fostering early academic career interests. Yet, most of my respondents did not freely use this terminology in their presentation of who inspired them most to pursue academic leadership. Ronald, the president at a public university, talked about how he did not have a formal mentoring plan. Ronald's friends, who did not have experience in higher education, served as his mentors:

> *I really haven't had any mentors and the reason is not so much because I think I know everything. The reason is more because I never – remember I said I never had any plan. Like to have a mentor, you've got to be trying to get somewhere. Like, well, she was my mentor because she helped me how to figure out how to get a job as a dean or how to do ... well, I was never trying to go anywhere. [...] I have people that I've learned*

things from. ... probably most of them would be more like friends. But, friends that I have a great deal of respect for their opinion. And, I have a friend that I've had since fifth grade, it's my closest friend in the world and – and he owned an executive recruiting firm and has never been, I mean, he graduated from college – but, he's never had one thing to do with higher ed. But, I would listen to [name of friend] when it came time to issues of personnel before I'd listen to anybody, anywhere. And, I'd call him and ask him questions. I'd say – I've got this problem with such and such and so and so and he taught me a lot.

The majority of my respondents talked about the importance of "role models" (Merton, 1968). They often learned from the successes and failures of others in addition to "on the job" training.

LEARNING FROM SUCCESSES AND MISTAKES OF OTHERS AND SELF

Mentorship can also occur in a different manner, via role models and this became apparent through my interviews (Gibson, 2004; Jung, 1986). Role models may be positive or negative, global or specific, close or distant, or up or across/down. Positive/negative role modeling refers to either valuing the beneficial outcomes of a role model's work or devaluing the unsatisfactory achievements (Gibson, 2004). Global/specific role modeling refers to valuing a collection of positive traits or just a few positive skills. Structurally, close/distant role modeling refers to personal relationships or role modeling from afar. Lastly, up and across/down role modeling refers to the hierarchical arrangement between the role model and the observer/follower.

Sometimes, respondents reported that their role models were more senior individuals under whom they had the opportunity of working at some point in their career. These role models did not necessarily have a personal relationship with the less senior administrators. At times, respondents reported that their role models were individuals that they had never met; respondents talked about how they admired the leadership of individuals whom they may have encountered or observed.

LEARNING FROM OTHERS' LEADERSHIP STYLE

Respondents often reported that they learned how to lead from close observations of their superiors during earlier parts of their careers. Through university committee involvement and firsthand monitoring of university, local, and national periodicals' reporting of administrators' job performance, respondents at early stages of their faculty careers spoke about witnessing exceptionally noteworthy examples of virtuous leadership. The respondents spoke about global matters relating to how their role models approached their jobs through a variety of tactics in addition to more specific traits in especially trying circumstances (Gibson, 2004).

For example, Bradford, a dean at a private university, credits a former professor as serving as his first role model who inspires his way of approaching his work:

> *He had tremendous integrity and spine and courage and he operated by his principles and he made it all look simple. In fact, any time I would see him compromise or do less than what he felt was right*

> *I would think oh, he compromised. In fact [...] his portrait hangs in a stairway at the college and I have a colleague who still goes and sits by it sometimes. This guy had a melanoma when he was 28, came back and he died at 53. So, there's a certain martyr thing in there too and he knew his whole life that he probably was going to die of cancer and as a result, he was the most focused human being I've ever seen.*

On the other hand, Emily, a provost at a public university, talked about how she did not have one particular role model or mentor. Instead, throughout her career as a teacher, scholar, and leader, she modeled the behavior of individuals for whom she had great admiration.

> *I wouldn't say that there was anyone who I viewed really as a mentor as much as I just looked around and watched what people did and the people who I modeled – tried to model – probably didn't even know I existed. You know, I was just watching them and observing how they behaved, how they made – at least what I could see about how they made decisions – how they treated people.*

Sophia, an associate provost at a private university, was especially perceptive of and respectful of her current provost's overall style in relation to policy enforcement.

> *For example, my current provost has this style where he – it will look like he's being completely waffling – but, what he's really doing is he's saying – well, let me hear you out. And, rather than reacting by saying no we can't do that – he says, well tell me what it is that you're asking about [...] if I can do*

this for you – I need to figure out how I can do this for everybody. So, I really admire his way of not hitting people over the head with his authority [...] he calls it the tai chi approach.

Sophia also spoke of how she looks up to the current president as a role model given the way in which he engages the Board of Trustees who as is often the case, a group of non-academics.

Our President has this amazing way of engaging the Board of Trustees. It's like a clinic in leadership. And, interestingly it doesn't – he's not necessarily as comfortable with the faculty – it's a different relationship and the faculty members are like openly hostile sometimes. [...] And then – so, then he sort of emceed this discussion and what he'll do and this is he always does it this way – he'll call on people – and say well you know [name of woman] said this and I'm hearing you say that [name of man #1] and I think there's some connection here. And, [name of man #2], I bet you've got something that – after [name of man #2] raised his hand – I bet you've got something that directly ties to both of those cause you have this experience in that. You know, he makes everybody feel like he's engaged and listening and like what they have to say matters.

Likewise, Paul, the president of a private liberal arts college, had a similar experience. He addressed the value in learning something from everyone he encounters, especially current and former college presidents.

I would say when I was a faculty member at [a previous institution]; the President of [that institution] was very supportive. He thought I had a real career. He encouraged me; he provided opportunities for me. But, he also believed in me and that was huge for me. He was someone I really admired and he wanted to see me succeed. He was one. Another was [name of President of another institution]. He is a very close friend of mine. I've known him a long time. And, he has supported me all along in advising me. [...] And, it goes back a long way starting with not graduate school per say but when I began my faculty career that were helpful to me as well and believed in me and gave me advice and so forth. I try to learn from everyone. I don't know where I learned this a long time ago. Someone said everybody you meet should teach you something no matter how unlikely that may seem.

Paul also acknowledged that while some of his leadership skills evolved from solid role modeling from individuals who were more senior to him, he continues to learn from his peers:

These are lonely jobs and it's often difficult to find on this campus people you can talk with about everything. It's just the way it goes. So, I have over the years developed friends who do this job as well. They're the ones that are probably most helpful because they know exactly what I'm talking about when I describe a budget challenge or a faculty challenge. [...] They're all either presidents or former presidents for the most part.

Similarly, Jake, the provost at a private university, spoke about how he admired his colleague's demeanor in meetings:

> *There was a guy, a faculty member at the school where I was who was fantastic in meetings. And, it took me about a year to understand what it was that he did that made meetings work well. And, I don't think that since then I've really changed very much. I mean – his style was to listen and listen and listen and out of the craziness of 8,000 people having different opinions to figure out so really there are really only just three major issues that we're all talking about and I think that's still what it is that I try to do in dealing with people. That is, to take the raw material of all the different ideas that people have and reduce them to a couple of questions that are actionable.*

Jake also addressed his respect for the current president of his institution given that he has the foresight to care about the institution's long-term prosperity:

> *His decision that we were going to scale back how much of the endowment we use per year. If he hadn't done it, no one would have realized he hadn't done it. [...] It made his life harder as president, much harder because he had less money to spend each year. You know, it's a lot easier to be president or provost if you could just tell people all the time – sure that's cool, do that – here's some money. So, to not do it because you are thinking of the health of the community 50 years from now, that's brave, I think.*

Stella, the president of a private university, specifically talked about one man who was in a senior leadership role that she often would think about when tackling challenges. Instead of contacting that person as she confronted perplexing tasks, she would ask herself how that individual would react and it helped her to pattern her actions.

> *[Name of man] was a great mentor and is still a great role model; he's the President of [name of university]. [...] And, I still just admire the way he would navigate those really challenging issues and I do find myself thinking what would [name of man] do? [...] Or, be proud of myself when I feel like I've done something that would be like the way [name of man] would do it.*

Respondents also cited historical or literary figures as role models that did not have direct ties to university leadership. Martha, a dean at a public university, talked about strong women in politics and public service such as Madeleine Albright, Mother Teresa, and Hillary Clinton who inspired her.

> *I always look for strong women who are able to mobilize groups of people for a good, common cause and create – you know – some way of people agreeing.*

Marcus, the provost at a public university, also spoke about his reverence for individuals in public leadership roles such as Martin Luther King Jr. and Thomas Jefferson and how he looks for quotes from them to inspire him. Similarly, Sabrina, the president of a public university, talked about how Nelson Mandela's leadership is a source of inspiration. Years ago, she and her husband had the opportunity to visit South Africa and she describes her interaction with a local Afrikaner that helped her understand the impact of the people's confidence in Mandela's authentic leadership:

> *I admire Mandela as a leader. I once went to South Africa the year after apartheid was eliminated and*

> *I was very interested in what the people had to say about apartheid and about the change cause I thought, my God, the whites must be really upset because the power is now being given to the blacks. And, so I went into a bar with my husband and … a man sat next to me. I asked him about the transition. And, he was an Afrikaner and you know he talked about how hard it was …. And then I said to them, why didn't the whites go up in arms, why wasn't there a revolution? How could this be done so peacefully? And, he said because we trust Mandela, there's only one person in the world who could have done this, he said and that was Mandela. And, I said, why do you trust him? And, he said because he always keeps his word. […] So, that's been a hallmark of my presidency. If I tell you I'm going to do something, I do it. If I can't do it, I tell you why I can't do it.*

On the other hand, William, a dean at a public university, talked about how a literary figure in a book series by C. S. Forester about a Napoleonic ship captain, that he had read as a child inspired his leadership approach.

> *He's very smart – smarter than the other people around him most of the time. But he is, and he commands this ship in battle and … on the inside, he always can see kind of all of the things that can go wrong with everything that's going to happen. So, as he's sailing into battle, he's imagining his ship being destroyed or even worse, him being horribly injured, but not killed and then a figure of fun by everybody. And, so on the inside you know he's filled with kind of doubt and insecurity – but, he has studied how he thinks heroic Napoleonic*

> *ship captains should act .... And, so on the outside, that's how he acts. And, he's calm under fire and you know, if there's an opportunity to do something brave even though he's terrified by the prospect, he tries to do the brave thing and he gets himself into trouble by speaking up and proposing sort of novel ideas. [...] And the result is – you know – that even though on the inside he's sort of – spends half of his time terrified – by acting like a brave heroic, Napoleonic ship captain, he actually becomes one. [...] The other thing he does...– there's a big battle and afterwards when he's reporting to the admiral ... he basically gives all the credit to his subordinates and his goal is to see them promoted and recognized for their accomplishments and not to sort of claim the rewards for himself. And... he's the person who kind of takes the ultimate responsibility even if somebody on his ship screws up.*

This example echoes themes of effective leadership that I addressed earlier: engaging the team, supporting the work of others, and sharing in the credit to build team morale.

Learning how to lead means watching and learning how others lead from a variety of domains and familiarity. On the contrary, it is just as important to have "non-role models" whose disastrous leadership serves as a reminder of how not to lead.

THE NON-ROLE MODEL: LEARNING FROM MISTAKES

Many leaders pointed out "non-role models" whose leadership style was in complete opposition to how they chose to lead. Sabrina, the president of a public university, spoke frankly about a former leader whose leadership style demonstrated to her how not to lead.

> *I worked for a woman, who I said, "Oh my god, if I ever become a president I don't ever want to be anything like her because she was so mean. She was just so mean, a bad temper and she always ascribed the worst motives to everybody. And, so she would be vindictive. If you for example were in a meeting and you said something critical of her or her policy, she would remember that and the next time she could sock it to you, she would sock it to you.*

Sophia pinpointed a vice president that she had worked for who blatantly disrespected a colleague by calling her the wrong name[1]:

> *[…] one of my staff members who is on this floor – there's a vice president that she works with regularly – her name is Alyssa and the vice president sent her an e-mail and said Dear Alice – and it just erased years of work that had been built up. That person has no clue how much sort of capital he or she just lost because Alyssa now knows – you don't really know who I am.*

Matthew, a dean at a private university, also talked about a situation in which the Provost's poor leadership taught him some important lessons about one's tactics in intervening in highly controversial matters.

> *[…] there were a bunch of curricular reforms that the Provost was trying to produce and I would say that she did not understand how to operationalize them and managed even to alienate allies because of*

picking fights over the wrong issue so an issue for instance of departmental integrity in hiring came up. She thought they hired somebody stupid but approached it in a way that raised the general issue of departmental, disciplinary superiority in judging.

Samuel, a dean at a private liberal arts college, talked about components of the current president's and a former president's leadership styles that he chose not to emulate in his working manner. Samuel addressed how aspects of the current president's more corporate leadership style were unbeneficial:

his Wall Street side comes in and I just think he's an idiot when he behaves that way. It just doesn't match this culture. So, saying things like somebody comes in and says, "I'm feeling like I'm not going to get everything done" and having the response be – "I pay a fair wage, get it done" is probably not quite [right] ....

Samuel also commented on a former president's ineffective leadership, marked by having values that did not match institutional values.

Her biggest problem was – and it really stopped the college and it stopped her – was overreaching. She was a person given to seeing – I'll use a different metaphor – she's leading, we're following – and she has walked so far ahead of us that no one can see her anymore. So, you can't follow her. In fact, if you knew where she was going, you might not want to follow her because it's pretty treacherous where she's headed. So, I think overreach was one piece. [Name of president] was a person who [betrayed] her own

> *gender in some pretty odd ways. So, she would flirt with male students in certain ways to try to get them to do things – not an individual student – but, she'd get in front of the Student Government Association and you would be almost ashamed to see the way she would behave and then realize that what she was doing was trying to get the guys to behave in a certain way. I saw her once walk up to a young student who was smoking and she walked up and she said you know "smoking will keep you from getting erections." This was the President of the college.*

Samuel did acknowledge that some of this former president's overreaching was beneficial to the college resulting in new programs and centers that are still in existence. However, this president was overall, not in touch with the feelings and needs of her constituency, which oftentimes resulted in some fairly awkward encounters.

Anna, a provost at a public university, spoke more globally about matters pertaining to how others lead that she has observed and found to be detrimental. Broadly speaking, Anna listed the following qualities as indicative of ineffective leadership:

> *Inability to make decisions, inability to resolve conflicts, inability to stick to a budget, inability to say no, inability to be honest and even if it sometimes means hurting someone's feelings or saying difficult things – lack of courage – the list goes on.*

Steven, a provost at a public university, also talked in a comprehensive way about a variety of qualities that he has seen in individuals that make them unsuitable for role model status.

> *They're poor communicators, they're very insular; they do not like to be outside of their comfort zone. And they react rather than be proactive and you know at the end of the day, based on all of those things that I said, one may come to the thought that maybe that person just didn't have the intellectual capacity and I would say that's not always true. Some of these individuals have tremendous intellectual capacity but not having had the experience or the comfort to be a good public speaker prevented them or in some cases really accelerated their inward-looking perspective.*

Mentoring, the academic experience itself, and learning what others do well and don't do well all inform effective leadership. Yet, actually being in the trenches also proves to be highly important for learning effective leadership.

"YOU HAVE TO EAT THE NOODLES": MUDDLING THROUGH AND LEARNING ON-THE-JOB

Respondents addressed how they found that it was not until they were actually "on the clock" that they truly learned the ins and outs of how to lead. Since many of these individuals had no formal academic training in leadership, they approached their time in their positions as hands-on learning experiences. My respondents may have been world-renowned scholars in their disciplines; however, their previous scholarship and research, for the most part, did not prepare them for what they would face in administrative roles. Through being in the middle of controversies and surprise situations, listening to the institution's diverse stakeholders with variant interests, and overcoming a fair number of mistakes, leaders learned how to lead best.

In an ever-changing university environment, Isabella, an associate provost at a public university, discussed how she approached challenges requiring immediate responses:

I have a close colleague in the office. [...] She started a couple of months before I did and so she kind of helped me get the lay of the land a little bit. We have a great staff here. I asked them a lot of questions. And, you sort of figure it out as you go. [...] And so, even to this day, you wouldn't believe the stuff that comes up so every day, there's [...] a new surprise, something you didn't know was coming. [...] So, there is no training for this. You figure out who you can trust and who's smart and you ask them. But, it's a very much figure-it-out-as-you-go-along kind of job.

Stanley, a dean at a public university, had a similar assessment of learning leadership:

Most of us who are administrators in the university setting came into that role as a faculty member and strangely enough most of us don't have a whole lot of training in management although we become managers and leaders. So, that varies a little bit by area. The people who have been in the business world have perhaps had more preparation and training in a formal way to be a manager because they've taken coursework and they've worked in the business world.

Given Stanley's statement regarding the academic origins of most university administrators, some respondents reported that they consulted an executive coach when they had come to a standstill in approaching a difficulty. Cynthia, the dean at a private liberal arts college, described a situation in which there was intense resistance from her direct reports. The situation was so severe that she decided to hire a coach:

I had a sort of insurrection from some people who report to me who [...] did not want to change. And, it was pretty ugly. So, how did I approach it? I got a coach. I told my boss, look here's what we need to do and clearly what I'm trying to do which is to try to cheerlead people into being able to think about what we need to do differently is not working. So, I got a coach, did a huge amount of work. Did a huge amount of reading. Worked with her to develop strategies and just little things like make sure you always take your secretary to lunch once a month. [...] And, I also knew that I wanted somebody, like it's a little bit like going for counseling. I wanted someone whose job it was to want to make me successful. So, somebody who would tell me hard things that didn't have any emotional attachment to me or any need to pull any punches [...].

Similarly, William, a dean at a public university, talked about how he learned that while as a faculty member, freedom of expression against administrative decisions was a highly valued tenet, as an administrator such behavior was unfavorable.

The President was doing something that none of the deans really thought was a good idea – actually nobody really thought it was a good idea – in fact, it was a terrible idea and I was organizing sort of the lobbying effort against it and I learned that as a dean you are not supposed to be sort of organizing

> *your fellow deans to rise up in opposition to the higher administration – they don't like that. And that's basically what I was doing. [...] And, actually I got in trouble with the Provost – I don't think he necessarily disagreed with us ... what he said to me in between the – you idiot, never do anything like this again was – every document at the university is public and if something like this ends up in the newspaper, you can really embarrass the whole university and one of the things you give up if you're going to be dean and have a nice big office is – you really are expected to support the university and if you have a problem with that, you should quit.*

Nicholas, a president of a private liberal arts college, also talked about the value of learning on the job. He addressed how he often helps less senior presidents when they call him for advice. Yet, he also acknowledged how the real learning does not take place until one personally champions through a difficult situation. For some challenging situations, such as the loss of students or faculty members, he felt that there is no training that could have prepared him for how to react in emergencies. Nicholas discussed one of those incredible challenges.

> *I had a murder-suicide inside the residence halls when I was President of [name of school] and there's no training, there's no bibliography. There's nothing to prepare you for making those calls to the parents and coping with that. You just have to make very sure that you are surrounded by very very competent people because there's no panacea. It's like the fire at [name of institution] years and years ago and how in the world do you wake up if you're president and you've got*

*five kids who are burned to death. There's no
training for that. There's no Harvard seminar on
the presidency that's going to tell you, well here's
what you should do when you have to make those
calls to the parents. So, if you're surrounded by
really good people, you'll make it through the
crises. But, those crises are the darkest moments
of any presidency. Losing a kid. It's the worst. It's
like what's the worst thing that can happen to a
parent? Losing a kid.*

Lisa, a dean at a private university, also addressed the importance of learning through on-the-job challenges and referenced a personnel related matter when she was a junior professor.

*And, I do think that in reading about literature and
what causes people to grow in it – in leadership or
in life – you've got to – you have to do challenging
things. So, looking back now, that was an
absolute gift. At the time, it was horrible, but that
experience probably contributed to my success; in
fact, I know it contributed to my success. […]you
have to eat the noodles – meaning, you've got to do
the hard stuff. If you don't do the hard stuff, you're
not going to grow; you're not going to develop.
You're not going to be able to do what you need to
do when it gets hard.*

Firsthand experience of the challenges of a higher educational institution also means knowing that while predecessors may have operated in a certain way when they held administrative positions, the change of leadership marks the start of a new regime.

PREDECESSORS

Learning "the ropes" and muddling through means that an administrator sees firsthand the challenges that are at hand and decides how best to respond. Paul's "insufferably arrogant" predecessor, as president of a private liberal arts college, for example, was not a beneficial guide. He had to decide for himself how to respond to the faculty and student concerns. Furthermore, Laura, a president at a private liberal arts college, charted a new direction when she took over as president after the leadership of a career administrator who did not put the needs of the college in highest esteem. Nicholas, a president at a private liberal arts college, had an exceptionally profound response to my question of whether or not his predecessor helped him at all with learning his position:

> *The best gift a president can give to his or her successor is to get the hell out of Dodge, never interfere, never intrude, and never go back. Go back for funerals and inaugurations and then only when asked. That's just a hard and fast rule of American higher education. And, I believe that 1,000 percent. You need to get out of the way.*

While he had contended with a difficult predecessor, Paul, the president of a private liberal arts college, was open to being a sounding board for his incoming successor. At the time of the interview, he was transitioning out of his position as president and preparing for a new presidency. As such, he reported benefitting from the open dialogue that he had established with his predecessor at his new institution.

> *And she and I have had a dream collaboration. She understands the job as I do. We're both seasoned presidents. We have a lot of respect and affection*

> *for one another [...] I was on the phone with her till I came out here to see you. She was having a senior staff meeting and asked me to join the call cause there were some issues that were relevant to me, and I think it has been a model of collaborative transition.*

For the purposes of the transition, it is helpful to have a cooperative predecessor. Stella, the president of a private university, addressed her dissatisfaction with the lack of assistance with the transition that she received from her predecessor:

> *[Name of predecessor] didn't help me at all. It was not an easy departure for him. I'll just put it that way.*

While incoming administrators generally welcome some help, it is unwelcoming to have a predecessor who wants to keep reins on the responsibilities of the position. Denise, the president of a private liberal arts college, also addressed the value of having insights from a predecessor given that it can help a leader to be prepared for challenges that lie ahead. Yet, Denise also noted that some personnel matters, for example, that a predecessor may have faced might not replicate themselves under a new presidency:

> *Part of what's interesting and what's good about getting his [her predecessor's] take on things is that you do realize that all problems and relationships are specific to the individuals in them.*

Overall, the ideal predecessor/successor relationship would be a mutually agreed upon open dialogue in which the successor can ask questions and the predecessor can respond specifically to those questions. The predecessor might warn of foreseeable difficulties that may pose problems for the entering administrator; however, that should be the extent of the exchange. After that, the successor, as Nicholas blatantly noted above, should withdraw from university proceedings so as to avoid stepping on the toes of the novel leader. Leaders need space to establish their own pathways that they develop after listening to the stakeholders, without worrying about imposing changes that may displease past administrations.

LISTENING AND LEARNING TO LEAD

Besides experiencing challenges and living through crises, learning how to be an effective leader involves listening. For example, it is important to listen to the stakeholders of an institution before making a major decision that may not be in line with the culture of the institution. Paul, the president of a private liberal arts college, listened to the student population's concerns over a racially insensitive building on campus. Frederick, the president of a private university, listened to his students when they expressed concerns over a variety of issues, including student group controversies as well as campus eyesores. Furthermore, Bradford, a dean at a private university, and Rachel, a provost at a public university, noted the importance of listening to and acknowledging diverse viewpoints from faculty who come from different disciplinary backgrounds. Listening to the stakeholders of an institution is one of the most important qualities for effective leaders to possess and also offers the most reliable method for leaders to learn how best to lead. Furthermore, institutional cultures change, making a pure reliance on predecessors' advice an incomplete strategy.

Maria, William, and Candace, all deans at public universities, each describe the importance of listening as a key method of leadership learning. As Maria noted:

> *[It is] important to listen, to really hear people. That means suspending whatever your own definitions of a situation are and that's sometimes difficult. But, so oftentimes, the problems that come our way are because people simply need to be heard and they're not feeling heard.*

William talked about the need to listen to one's advisors as a leader given that there will be instances in which one is called to make a decision on an issue where one might not be an expert:

> *But, you know, we have professionals here with MBAs who do this. And, the most important thing is to listen to them. And, if they say – "I really don't think that's a good idea – you shouldn't do that." Then, don't do it.*

Similarly, Candace talked about recognizing the importance of listening given one's limited understanding of situations. A dean cannot possibly know everything that is going on within the college:

> *Then, you have to listen to people. You don't know everything. You have to talk to everybody who has something to do with whatever issue you're trying to do something about. And, that requires that you're the type of person who can talk to other people. And, you know, get their opinions.*

A leadership training, workshop, or seminar may help a current or incoming leader learn the importance of listening to institutional stakeholders; however, that training cannot prepare the leader for the exact stakeholder motivations. By having "eaten the noodles" and muddling through one's positional responsibilities, a leader learns what it means to lead.

FORMAL LEADERSHIP TRAINING

Leaders also learn how to lead by attending workshops and seminars. The sessions that respondents most often reported attending were specifically geared toward academic administrators. Sometimes respondents attended these trainings because the institution specifically recommended that they attend them. Other times, the respondents personally sought them out. For others, they were sorry to not be able to attend trainings since circumstances were such that they jumped right into their positions with little time for leadership reflection. In such circumstances, executive coaches can fill this void. Some respondents also spoke of their experiences in attending gender-specific leadership trainings.

BENEFITS OF FORMAL LEADERSHIP TRAINING

Sophia, a provost at a private university, who had a very intentional career path without much research or teaching experience beyond graduate school, was exceptionally delighted by the awareness that she developed through her participation in a leadership training program that was not just geared for academic administrators and spoke highly of the exercises she engaged in there.

> *My job was to persuade other people to behave in a certain way. And, if I could persuade them – then I could achieve a goal. If I was right, I wasn't achieving a goal. […] And, then after the game we talked about the fact that –* are we one organization? Or, are we five competitors? *Because if you see yourself as five competitors, then if one group wins at the expense of the others, you may*

have actually won. But, if you're one organization, and one subunit within the organization wins at the expense of the others, that's not a win, that's a loss.

Marcus, a provost at a public university, also spoke enthusiastically about his leadership training experience back when he was transitioning into his present role.

I knew I was starting in early July of that year and before I began I contacted this institution and I said, I know I'm just starting this job, but I notice that this workshop is being offered and I'd really like to go. And they said – by all means – and what I liked about it in particular is they had us do a lot of scenarios and problem solving as a group. So, for example, they would have four or five of us together at a table and say here's a personnel challenge of this difficult person is – and they would describe a hypothetical and have us solve it together and then share it with the broader group, so that was very useful.

Similarly, Louis, the provost at a public university, talked about how he has benefited from his attendance at leadership trainings. He attended one popular academic leadership training program at Harvard University earlier in his career and was involved in an ongoing, regional leadership training program. He saw networking as one of the prime benefits of these trainings.

So, the approach [at the Harvard trainings] was really kind of styles of leadership .... There was a book that we read and the authors were there. So, we got it from the horse's mouth and these were people who characterized different styles of

> *leadership. ..., they brought people that exemplified that kind of leadership including the President of [name of university], a woman who was a very charismatic person and then a woman who built a sense of community around. She was an emotive leader [...] and so we were kind of asked to situate ourselves on these various spectrums and I think the takeaway is that you have to be aware of all of them and you may be predominately this kind of leader, but that there are circumstances when you might embody some elements of the others or that you needed to and that there are circumstances. I mean one of my deans is gone because he could only be one kind of leader. And there were decisions that I needed made that were just not part of his repertoire.*

Clearly, Louis reported the many benefits of having the opportunity to attend this leadership training in the past. His strong recollection of details from the training, years after his attendance is a testament to its influence on his career.

Laura, the president of a private liberal arts college, talked about how she had benefited from attending Harvard leadership training for new presidents. Similar to Louis, Laura also noted the benefits of networking.

> *I went to the – you know Harvard does this program for new college presidents and I went to that the summer after I was appointed president and that was fantastic; it was great. And there is some leadership training embedded in that; it's also sort of content, you know, learning a little bit more about running a college. But, and lots of good connections with peers at other institutions who are also new presidents and I've been able to maintain*

> *some of those connections. They are people who you can once in a while pick up the phone and call. So, that's fantastic. So, that would be one. I went to – with our Board Chair – I went to an AGB[2] conference ... for board chairs and presidents and it really was focused on roles, the president, the chair, and the board. And, thinking about leading an institution and how you forge a partnership and do that together and I found that to be very helpful.*

Laura reported that after both of these conference experiences, she came away with a clearer vision about her role and responsibilities as a college president.

Rachel, a provost at a public university, also lauded her experience at past leadership trainings and noted the importance of how she expanded her network through these programs:

> *I believe the Harvard professional programs – and, I've completed two certificates, were essential to strengthening skills I had already developed and recognized that I had. But, they were very helpful in that I developed networks. The most important piece wasn't so much the books that we read as developing a network of peers and listening to their experiences of how things were done on their campuses.*

> *The second professional development program I attended at Harvard, persons were from throughout the world – it wasn't just the U.S. [...] So, it took on more of a global perspective. [...] We were all given this long reading list, which was a good thing because that's all we did. We were away*

> *from our campuses; we had an assignment before arriving and we read. We looked at a lot of case studies, lessons learned from case studies. So, that was important in that it strengthened my style of resolving and problem solving those issues from day to day. And, it also helped me to understand the transition between the role of a faculty member and an administrator.*

Eisenhardt (1989, p. 548) underscores the role that case study research plays in theory development: "Theory developed from case study research is likely to have important strengths like novelty, testability, and empirical validity, which arise from the intimate linkage with empirical evidence." As such, for higher educational leaders, particularly those without leadership based disciplinary interests; the case study approach enables them to learn from modules that are based on actual experiences. Leaders who are exposed to case studies can then employ the theories to develop their own approaches.

Samuel, a dean at a private liberal arts college, also talked about how his institution encouraged him to attend a leadership training and how much he benefited from that experience – so much so that he in turn later shared what he had learned with others.

> *When I was [an] associate dean [...] I went to – the Management Development Program – .... This one was aimed at people who were four or five years in a dean's role at the associate level. Perfect summer for me. The college both recommended it and paid for it and gave me the paid time off to do it so that I was absolutely encouraged here. I also participated in something called the American*

> *Council of Education's Chief Academic Officer's Forum – new chief academic officer's forum which is a series of meetings through the first year as chief academic officer. And, that worked out so well that I went back and taught at it twice.*

Samuel encourages all incoming leaders who are chairs of departments, for example, to attend workshops on leadership. Furthermore, he has found his experience to be so beneficial that he has chosen to give back to assist future leadership development through teaching at these sessions.

In contrast, Caroline, a president at a public university, had mixed feelings about the merits of leadership training. She broadly discussed the benefits and drawbacks of leadership trainings.

> *I went to the two-week thing at Harvard – the Institute for Educational Management. I went to the one for provosts. Yeah. It's all right. A lot of these programs are about the other people you meet and also for the Harvard program because you're there for two weeks and you stay there and they say do not do your email – get completely away from your home job – that's very valuable because even if all the classes aren't great and the faculty aren't great, it gives you a chance to reflect out of your regular environment. One of our deans just did the same program and he felt the same way I did about it, but he felt it was worthwhile because at least it spurred him to think about his own leadership because he was in this place away from the day-to-day hassles. So, some people get a lot out of that. Maybe, I just didn't go to the right program.*

Similarly, Isabella, a provost at a public university, expressed dissatisfaction toward the merits of leadership training. Isabella felt that on-the-job training was the only way to truly comprehend how to perform the duties of one's position:

> *Yes, I have been to academic leadership programs. They're a little frustrating. Not that they're not valuable. But, because a lot of academic leaders haven't had other careers, they tend to be geared towards people who haven't ever led people or supervised anybody. So, they're a little annoying because that's stuff that I was taught [in a previous leadership career]. [...] Somebody can tell you that you should talk this way or act this way, but until you try it and do it, you don't own it. It's not a classroom activity.*

Broadly, my respondents who reported that they had benefitted from leadership trainings most often cited that the most constructive aspects of the leadership trainings were the case studies. Often, higher educational administrators who had lived through and navigated such experiences in addition to the network-building opportunities led the case study exercises. Other highlights for my respondents included the opportunity to network with other administrators and their establishment of a clearer vision of the responsibilities of their leadership positions. On the other hand, respondents agreed that there is no substitute for on-the-job training. While hearing from another president, provost, or dean on how they resolved a crisis has its merits, firsthand undertakings are most instructive for leaders.

Indeed, there are a myriad of gender-specific leadership trainings that are now available for women. How do they address gendered leadership issues?

TRAINING FOR WOMEN: GENDER-SPECIFIC LEADERSHIP TRAINING

Gender-specific trainings have evolved from women's historical absence from leadership positions in all spheres as a result of systemic, gender-based marginalization. For example, Debebe (2009) studied women's transformational learning through women-specific leadership development training for scientists and managers. While she found that post-training, such formalized leadership training was advantageous, the only discernible reason for offering a separate venue for women was based on their historical absence from the field. While it is indisputable that women are underrepresented in many fields including STEM disciplines and administrative roles, it is also the case that gender, work, and organizations scholars (Bird, 2011; Bystydzienski & Bird, 2006; Mayberry, 2004) argue that women-centered approaches are inadequate. As such, systemic-wide training to address barriers for marginalized groups carries more merit (Bird, 2011; Connell, 2006; Czarniawska, 2008).

Training women how to lead and how to advance in their careers without addressing the role that men, who have largely held the positions of power within most major institutions, play in this endeavor therefore seems fruitless. Women in the workplace still confront the "old boys' network" (Wass & McNabb, 2006) and still shelter the burden of domestic work and care work (Eagly et al., 2003). Given these gendered experiences, the greatest merit in women-centered trainings appears to come from the women-specific networks that women create based on their interactions with other women who are confronting the "old boys' network" and traditional gender roles.

Some of my respondents who were women administrators reported that they seek out and welcome gender-specific leadership trainings. In addition, some of the men administrators reported supporting junior women's involvement in such trainings. On the other hand, other respondents reported their hesitancy toward such trainings.

For example, Candace, a dean at a public university, reported that she had attended a Higher Education Resource Services (HERS) Institute session, geared specifically for women. Candace reported:

> *Yes, it was [helpful]. It was an introduction to setting goals and to me that's the first thing that was noticeable. And, when I left – when I was done being part of the program, I realized and (I was interim dean that year) – the first thing to figure out was what I wanted to accomplish that year. You don't think about [matters like that] when you start, cause you figure, my goodness, I've never been dean, here I am being dean. And, okay, I'm here and what am I going to do? And, I'm going to accomplish something; I'm not going to just sit around' and so I did [...].*

I also asked Candace to clarify who was in attendance at the HERS Institute session that she attended:

> *There were women role models, there were some male you know facilitators and presenters, but they were primarily women involved because it is a women's leadership program and the women and the participants are women.*

For Candace, the positive takeaway from her women-specific leadership training was that she should begin her tenure as dean by figuring out her goals and that entailed speaking with her supervisor.

Gina, a dean at a public university, also reported her positive experience in participating in a yearlong women's empowerment leadership training, led by corporate chief executive officers, that was not through the HERS Institute, and that did not specifically focus on educational leadership.

> *So, all the people taking the course were women and almost all the people giving us the advice or giving us the lectures were men. It was really interesting so there were probably two or three women, four or five guys who came in to do different things and there was I think eight of us or ten of us and it took the place, it took the format of discussion sessions, roundtable discussions, the odd lecture scenarios presented to us and then we had to kind of respond. But, the most interesting thing about it was that everybody, all the women in the room in very different jobs all had the same jobs and the problems invariably were around people and that was the big issue was particularly when you see and again I don't find it so much here but I'm sure it exists here as well where you'd almost have men looking down on women and kind of feeling well you're not as good as us and it was learning how to deal with that through a whole different pile of scenarios and we acted out different situations, etcetera.*

Gina's account reflects that she was exposed to case studies that provided strategies for approaching instances in which men looked down on women for being in leadership positions. She also described her reservations about the leadership program while it was in progress.

> *And so, at the time I was kind of doing it and I felt this is all a bit of common sense and I am not sure that I'm learning a whole lot but actually just the fact of doing it and I would think it was the personal empowerment that it gave me that it was about you know you're not alone in this, this is not something that you're just not good at this is just another skill that you've got to learn how to deal with.*

Overall, she found the training to be constructive given that it helped her to establish a network among other administrators across a variety of fields. As such, this training fostered a sense of community that helped her realize the gendered dynamic of her experience.

Nadine, the president of a private liberal arts college, also talked about the benefits from participating in gender-specific leadership programs:

> *ACE [American Council on Education] has a series of programs to encourage women to go into leadership roles and I found those particularly valuable. And, when you're in the job, the job's the same but I think it was the encouragement from women in particular to go into some of the higher education administrative roles that I found encouraging and in turn […] I network with younger women; I'm no longer at the point where I'm going to workshops to learn about that next stage but I do go to workshops to help if I can play a role on a panel or help other women in particular advance or mentor women. And, so it's that kind of payback that always I think is very important. But, yeah, ACE, I'd strongly recommend their programs;*

> *they're very supportive of women. They've got strong women they're concerned that not enough women are going into higher education roles and so it's a great organization.*

Nadine demonstrates the value of mentorship and encouragement from other women in the field who inspire junior leaders to aspire toward more substantial roles.

Corrine, a provost at a private university, also reported having a positive experience at a women-centric leadership institute:

> *[One] that I've particularly found useful was the HERS Institute, which used to be run like a boot camp, like a five-week residential boot camp. But, it really helped me. It was structured so that there were units on the various facets of higher education administration. Finance, development and fundraising, faculty development, legal perspectives, student affairs kind of thing and that kind of helped me see for the first time beyond through the lens of my discipline, my faculty status, what the business of higher education is all about. And, I think that's a really important part of professional development is figuring out what game am I playing? And, is this the game I want to play?*

Corrine's positive experience at the HERS Institute did not necessarily reflect any gender-specific training that she found that she benefited from. Yet, Corinne did talk about her role in assisting women through leadership trainings in which she was a facilitator.

> *The training that I was doing and I have very little time to do anymore is very specific. And, it*

> *has to do with, I would suggest it's interpersonal communication, but it's physical, so it's nonverbal. [...] So, I talk to women a lot about inhabiting their physical realm and what that can do to help them actualize themselves in a work environment. Everything from becoming aware of vocal patterns, becoming aware of physical habits; how you carry yourself and how that might be interpreted nonverbally particularly in a male-dominated executive world. How much space you occupy, where you sit in a room – all of those are signifiers of power and in executive situations you're almost, somebody is always negotiating the power in the room, in the conversation. So, it's just a different way for women to have some awareness about what may or may not work for them.*

Corrine's assessment parallels scholarship on gender socialization and social role theory (Eagly, 1987; Eagly & Johannesen-Schmidt, 2001; Eagly et al., 2003; Eagly & Johnson, 1990; Eagly & Karau, 2002). Based on this understanding, women leaders may be more communal, collaborative, and deferential given their socialization. Earlier, I dismissed these perceptions of women's leadership in higher education and noted vast similarities between women and men in terms of leadership style that is marked by shared governance and transparency. Here, it is noteworthy that Corinne notes this difference in women's leadership by mentioning that women need to become aware of the messages that they have been socialized to send through their body language, for example. Corinne impacts women who are aspiring to hold executive leadership roles by reminding them that these social conventions are disadvantageous toward women's advancement and that they must reshape their responses to be respected.

All of the respondents, women and men, demonstrated an openness toward supporting leadership development through media that were suitable to others, whether its books, trainings, on-the-job training, or networking among colleagues and peers. There was a common understanding that certain individuals benefit from learning through particular media. Two men respondents specifically addressed their open support for women's participation in HERS Institutes if they chose to go down that path.

For example, William, a dean at a public university, talked about his support for department heads' training in general and for the HERS Institute that is specific to women. He stated:

> *There's something called the HERS Institute at Bryn Mawr which is for women who are interested in higher education leadership positions. I think we've probably sent somebody every year to that. But, there is no regular program; it's all on individual initiative.*

Similarly, Steven, a provost at a public university, talked about his support for women to attend gender-specific trainings in addition to more generalized training for women and men.

> *We have many deans who've attended the Harvard leadership forum that's held during the summer. We also sponsored women faculty members who aspire to become administrators through two different programs. One is called ELATE and that's run through Drexel University and the other is called the HERS Institute out of Bryn Mawr. So, we are promoting more of our faculty members to pursue that route. But, in academia we also have the ACE*

> *Fellows Program. [...] That's a great program where through – it's the American Council of Education and through that program aspiring administrators will be assigned to a senior administrator at another university. So, they get to work with that person and also see the day-to-day dealings. It's a great learning experience.*

William and Steven did not impose training upon junior colleagues; yet, they did note its availability. Lisa, a dean at a private university, reported that she confronted exceptional pressure to attend gender-specific leadership training and her resistance.

> *Starting this summer, I'm going through a yearlong leadership program for just women that the Provost has really encouraged me to go [to]. It's one-week trips, three times a year through the course of the year and it's women only. And, actually, that's something that I don't like about it. I don't want it to be just women.*

I probed further to find out why she had the aversion toward attending this program:

> *Because, I have a pretty good network of women. There have been groups of women getting together regularly in my discipline the whole time. So, maybe it's leadership, maybe it's bits and pieces that it's – I feel like I'm going to meet the women anyway. And, I could always just pick up the phone in fact I am planning on picking up the phone and calling the Provost at [name of nearby university] and seeing to meet. So, I'm going to meet them anyway and since the program I did here [a university leadership*

> *program for women and men at her present institution] was about the strongest thing was the cohort – the network you're going to have moving away from it, I didn't want my network to be just women. I wanted my network to be men and women. But, now that I'm going I'm going to make the most out of it.*

Lisa mentioned that she talked to others about her distaste for participating in women-centered leadership training and how she did receive some valuable input that helped change her mind:

> *Now, in my grumbling path about [name of program] being just for women, I did talk with somebody who said – who did give me a couple valuable things for it to be just women. That, while I said I could go reach out to these people, she said you're not going to because you don't have the time. You have to make the time. So, here's a way to make the time to do it.*

Lisa realized that while she may have every intention of networking in the midst of her demanding schedule, the likelihood of that happening is uncertain. Purposefully building time into her schedule to establish these networks then took on a different meaning for her.

Administrators take a variety of learning pathways to support their career growth. Through mentoring from senior administrators and peers at all stages of their careers, respondents reported that they benefitted from having a sounding board and a cheering section as they navigated their current and future careers. Respondents also indicated that by learning from others' successes and failures, they equipped themselves to face similar challenges. They would sometimes reflect back on an instance of model leadership when confronted with seemingly insurmountable challenges. On the other hand, they reflected on the failings of inept leaders as motivation for how not to lead. Respondents adamantly spoke of the necessity of learning on-the-job and learning from one's personal successes and failures.

Further, learning through leadership trainings proved to be an incredibly helpful avenue for respondents' experiences in understanding their approaches to their responsibilities. For those respondents who directly experienced gender-specific leadership training for women, the most salient component of the sessions was the opportunities for networking. Such a finding warrants further inquiry into the construction of gender-specific trainings for women that may evolve into networking and community building exercises for women who confront the "old boys' network" of executive administration.

Overall, these findings on women-specific leadership trainings shed light on the future foci of gender-specific leadership training. While the women respondents tended to acknowledge some benefit of gender-specific programing for women administrators, there was also some discomfort with the idea of these gendered and separate experiences. And they implied that the terminology of "women's training sessions" that we use for these programs suggests that women and men should be trained separately and that men who are not taking part in these women-centered trainings are already experts on what the women are learning in these settings. Such an implication promotes gender essentialism. What remains to be identified is what is to be gained, and what is lost, for both leaders and their institutions, in holding gender-specific training sessions, and, by contrast, more general, non-gender-specific sessions?

None of my respondents mentioned trainings or networking opportunities that were specific to other marginalized identities with respect to race, ethnicity, or sexuality.

While there is certainly an abundance of organizations that focus on supportive networks for individuals of marginalized statuses (e.g., National African-American Women's Leadership Institute, the Executive Leadership Council, LGBTQ Executive Leadership Program at Stanford University Graduate School of Business, and the Association of Latino Administrators and Superintendents), leadership is a trait that is gendered with binary categorizations, more than it is differentiated with respect to race, ethnicity, trans, nonbinary, or intersex identity, or sexuality, for example. Future research ought to look at how networks with the mission of uplifting individuals of marginalized statuses help leaders to navigate leadership.

In the next chapter, I focus on the social construction of leadership as a gendered phenomenon and shift attention to respondents' gendered experiences.

NOTES

1. I have changed the name of this individual. However, the similarity between the two names demonstrates the point.

2. AGB stands for Association of Governing Boards of Universities and Colleges.

4

GENDER AND LEADERSHIP IN HIGHER EDUCATION

Women have historically faced institutional barriers to advancement in the workplace (Acker, 1990, 1992; Bird, 2011; Britton, 1997, 2000; Lorber, 1984; Lovejoy & Stone, 2012; Martin, 2003; Morgan & Martin, 2006; Ridgeway, 1997; Williams, 1992, 1995). The gendered work structure constrains workers' dress, language, expressions, and actions to neatly fit into socially constructed masculine or feminine categories (Martin, 2003) that suit traditional gender roles (Butler, 1990; Eagly & Johannesen-Schmidt, 2001; Eagly et al., 2003; Eagly & Johnson, 1990; Eagly & Karau, 2002).

Just as there are tactics for approaching one's place in a non-traditional role with respect to gender (Eagly & Carli, 2007; Williams, 1992, 1995), there are consequences for crossing boundaries, such as reprimands from superiors and peers, promotion freezes, and termination that delineate gender-suitable work behavior given these roles (Castro, 2012; Hochschild, 1983; Lorber, 1994, 2000, 2005). Eagly and Karau (2002), Heilman and Okimoto (2007), and Katila and Eriksson (2013) confirm the negative consequences that result from women leaders' non-communal practices and suggest how women can diminish prejudice through altering their leadership styles. Eagly and Karau (2002) find that if women were to become more communal and taper their agentic qualities, "the existing female gender role would become more congruent with leader roles, and female leaders should experience decreased prejudice and increased acknowledgment of their effectiveness" (p. 591). Similarly, Brescoll (2011) revealed that women who are exceptionally voluble or portray anger face damaging consequences that might subsequently upset their advancement.

Given these findings, what role does gender play in the narratives of women and men leaders in higher education? Furthermore, once women have attained positions of authority as deans, provosts, and presidents, do these same gendered barriers still haunt them as they might have throughout their ascendancy toward these top administrative positions?

I asked my respondents if they could identify a time in their careers in which others responded to them less for being a president, dean, or provost and more because of their gender. I also probed for insights on their observations on the gendered treatment of others in administrative leadership posts, especially if the respondents indicated that they had never felt that their own gender identities had ever influenced their interactions. Key themes that emerged from the interviews relate to the gendered work and family balance and traditional gender roles and gender and power.

SOCIALLY CONSTRUCTED GENDERED LEADERSHIP GENDER ROLES

Socially constructed gender expectations imply women's justification for their placement in a particular leadership role by comparing their organizational or oversight duties to traditional gender roles for women, including housekeeping or child rearing. Women are accountable for "emotional labor" (Hochschild, 1983) via more nurturing and subservient workplace roles such as remembering birthdays and listening to associates' personal problems (Kanter, 1977; Martin, 2003; Pierce, 1995). While leaders are often accountable for at least minimal emotional laboring and communality, this scholarship underscores gendered expectations that women confront. Furthermore, Ollilainen and Calasanti (2007) suggest how metaphors pertaining to gendered family roles are sustained, often unconsciously, in self-managing teams with men and women workers. This finding parallels earlier research regarding the role that social role theory (Eagly, 1987; Eagly & Johannesen-Schmidt, 2001; Eagly et al., 2003; Eagly & Johnson 1990; Eagly & Karau, 2002) plays in contributing to a gendered hierarchy within the workplace; this workplace hierarchy mimics interactions that we find in private, domestic spheres.

Three respondents spoke of specific examples in which they either experienced or witnessed differential treatment as a result of traditional understandings of women's gender roles. Rachel, a provost at a public university, offered a poignant example of a time in which she, a woman of color, confronted backlash associated with traditional gender roles at a national conference. In this particular case, an older white man who was serving as provost at another institution made an assumption about Rachel's ability to contribute.

> *We were in small groups and someone – we were told someone has to serve as a scribe. So, this older provost, male – looked at me and said, "Oh, well you can serve. You can take the notes, can't you?" What was my response? A non-response.*

> *I continued to do primarily because what he thought and the others said – "why don't you?" So, he then said – "well, you won't be able to read my handwriting." Well, how would he know that my handwriting would be legible? So, this is still very much entrenched and this guy was a much older provost.*

Rachel resisted this gender role to serve the group in this "housekeeping" capacity via note-taking services. Often, in a group situation, the note-taker listens and is so consumed with diplomatically recording group contributions that it limits the note-taker's substantive involvement.

On a related note, Cynthia, a dean at a private liberal arts college, noted a past work environment at another higher educational institution that was hostile and demeaning toward non-submissive women. Her experience being treated as an inferior with an expectation that she could easily be manipulated by the more senior administrators parallels gendered understandings that women will be submissive to men of authority. When I asked Cynthia if she had ever been treated differently because of her gender, she stated:

> *I felt like every day. [It was a] very male place. […] One of the reasons I left was because the then provost who I did not respect, called me into his office and shouted at me and threatened my job and asked me how I would behave differently in the future. You know, unbelievably belittling.*

Cynthia's experience depicts how a clash of gendered understandings of how women ought to behave conflicts with a patriarchal social construction that mandates women's subservience. Similarly, Marcus, the provost at a public university, noted that he had observed others' disparaging comments at his previous institution where there is a woman president. There, stakeholders disagreed with the president's decisions by comparing her role to that of a queen.

> *There still were those who when they disagreed with her or they didn't like her approach, they would be derogatory of female things. Like, they would say she's being a queen, things like that. And, I remember when I heard those comments, I thought well, she's the leader, she's supposed to be the one who's making the [decision] – you may not like it.*

Furthermore, Paul, a president at a private liberal arts college, also noticed gendered differences, rooted in traditional understandings of gender roles, among the way in which his peers talked about the incoming woman president's inability to attend a meeting.

> *She was not able to come to some meeting for something and I remember somebody saying well, she's a mom, she's got a lot of stuff to deal with. And, I remember saying it doesn't have anything to do with it. She's going to be the President; she's going to have to deal with it. That isn't why she's not here today but nobody's going to cut her a break because she's a mom. She's a president first in this job.*

Paul also commented on perceived challenges that he felt that women leaders in higher education have with regard to matters concerning athletics:

> *I know for instance a colleague at an elite university who is dealing with an athletic issue and in the end, she just didn't do it because she didn't have*

> *the same credibility that a man would have. If she were to take a hard line on athletics, it would be a war because who is she to do it, she doesn't even understand it because she's a woman and that may play itself out in certain kinds of issues where women are seen or have greater challenges because the gender issue is seen to be important.*

Taken together, these above observations indicate a pattern of underlying gender role perceptions and expectations of women in the workplace that mirror socially constructed gender roles.

THE WORK AND FAMILY BALANCE

I did not explicitly ask about respondents' management of work and family nor did I probe about family matters. Yet, this theme that gender scholars (Acker, 1990, 1992; Cha, 2013; Damaske, 2011; Gerson, 2010; Hochschild, 1997; Kelly, Ammons, Chermack, & Moen, 2010; Macdonald, 2010; Williams, 2010) have identified as prominent with regard to gendered workplace experiences became apparent in my data analysis. Serving as a dean, provost, or president often warrants round-the-clock availability to respond to crises and to attend to the high volume of work. Daytimes may be reserved for in-person meetings and events. As such, respondents reported a blurring of the boundary between work time and family time that required an ongoing balancing act.

Women, much more often than men, talked about managing familial responsibilities in addition to their professional responsibilities. Yet, men also recognized strategies for managing their work and family lives. While women and men both expressed these challenges, women respondents identified more significant challenges as they managed their personal and public personae. And while none of my respondents spoke of not having children or partners as a way of limiting the strains of managing a work and family balance, some of my women respondents did speak of the convenience of delaying leadership to a time when their children were grown. Furthermore, scholarship also confirms that women who do not have children will statistically have higher salaries (Cheung & Halpern, 2010). As such, it makes sense that while some of my women respondents addressed the challenges of the work and family balance, they also noted that having older children who did not require as much of their attention made for an easier decision to take on a leadership role. Notably, none of my men respondents made this observation.

Both Joanne, a provost at a private liberal arts college, who was hesitant to take on a key leadership role given that she had a young child at home, and Anna, a provost at a public university, talked about the "right time" for a leadership position when one is on an academic career track that offers flexible work hours. Anna noted her leadership pathway:

I had been asked to come into a vice provost role a couple of times, but I was struck between the need to be a good mother and to put my kids' needs ahead of my own and my own love for my research.

Yet, years later when the position was available again, Anna had even more experience at that point, her children were older, and an administrative position felt more manageable for her. Anna reported that she works about 12 hours a day and that she always works on Sunday evenings. Anna did not perceive that she could have been as committed to this position earlier on in her career even with the help of her husband who also has a demanding career. Anna did not address whether or not her husband made similar compromises when the kids were small with regard to work responsibilities. Corinne, the provost at a private university, also acknowledged that, in particular for women, it is much easier to serve in such a time-consuming leadership role once one's children are grown.

> *I am and I think most women, particularly, in a position like this have to be total workaholics and I think I made a conscious decision that this would be a priority. I also made some decisions, as my children grew older that I can then assume larger and more demanding roles.*

Here, Corinne draws a gendered distinction. Women, who are of an advanced age without school age children, for example, may have more flexibility to take on leadership roles than younger women with younger children.

Rachel, the provost at a public university, also acknowledged how it is much easier to manage work and family responsibilities once children are either adults or at an age of substantial maturity. She stated:

> *my son's now an adult, so I'm not at that point in my career in my life – my personal life where that becomes – a really important issue that impacts what I do.*

Rachel did acknowledge that a way for women (and I would argue that this applies to leaders of all gender identities) to overcome situations in which they cannot be on time to a meeting as a result of family matters is simply by being productive.

> *When, I arrive late – I have to give credit to my colleagues who are all males – not a one makes a comment. But, generally, that's due to my diligence in getting there and establishing a record of getting*

> *there early. And, that's also because I'm aware of these kinds of existing nonsensical kinds of attitudes. But, it is – and individuals will say – it shouldn't happen but it is a part of the world we live in. And, the only way to respond to that again is simply by being productive.*

Leaders also face situations in which being productive is simply not going to resolve a work and family balance issue. Furthermore, familial responsibilities, of course, do not necessarily end when one's children are older. Sabrina, a president at a public university, recounted a graduation dilemma given that her daughter's medical school graduation was scheduled for the exact same day as the first graduation that she would host as president. Ultimately, Sabrina decided to choose family first and did not miss the opportunity to witness her daughter's milestone. I asked Sabrina if she felt that men face the same sort of challenge with regard to putting their job first over family matters. Sabrina addressed what she perceives to be differences between women and men leaders and their approaches to the work and family balance:

> *I think men face it, but I do think that they put their job first. I think there are men – there's always the exception – who would have done what I did. But, I would love to ask in a questionnaire, how many men would have done what I did. Cause I think, well the woman [a friend of hers who chose to skip her daughter's undergraduate commencement because of a work commitment] that I told you about at lunch, didn't do it. She just, she said she was terrified of losing her job by not going to commencement for her daughter. So, I think that females are more likely to you know, to say this is a family issue; my family comes first.*

While Sabrina's friend clearly did not put her family first and prioritized her job, Sabrina feels that more women than men are likely to put their foot down when their jobs require that they brush aside key family events. As such, given that women are commonly held to communal standards and are understood to be more socially responsible for keeping families functioning, they may confront the expectation that putting family first is not a novel idea. Had Sabrina not done what she did, individuals within the community may have even seen her as too business-minded, or overly agentic.

Women respondents, in particular, noted that leadership trainings for women offered a forum for discussing the challenges that women are more predisposed to confront given societal views on disproportionate women's roles in contributing to "second shift" labor (Hochschild, 1989). Caroline, a president at a public university, addressed the importance of gender-specific leadership trainings for women given that they provide the opportunity for women to talk about how they manage work and family.

> *I think it's great to have it be all women because we do have specific problems related to life cycle and children and all that stuff.*

Joanne, a provost at a private liberal arts college, echoed Caroline's thoughts with regard to the importance of women mentors in leadership roles given that women confront different issues than men confront based on socially constructed understandings of women's share of household labor. Caroline noted:

> *Both as an undergraduate and as a graduate student probably here on the faculty I would say that I probably was mentored more by female faculty than male faculty. And that also influenced*

discussions about life outside the college too – you know, insights about work-life balance and so forth. So, we certainly – one of the things we used to do at [name of present college] was pair female faculty assistant professors with tenured faculty and so I think that was part of the culture here for a while.

While women respondents spoke explicitly of exceptional challenges that they faced as a result of managing their demanding work responsibilities in addition to family responsibilities, men respondents acknowledged the work and family balance more abstractly: the challenge did not impact them to such an extent that they ever thought of putting off a promotion for the sake of their family's well-being. Paul, a president at a private liberal arts college, talked about his family commitment when he recounted his typical workday.

I tend to get up very early in the morning and exercise because if I don't do it then, it isn't happening. And then I spend a fair amount of time at home. I have breakfast with my family and I do emails and that kind of thing to get that stuff done. Then, I'm in the office typically between 8:30 and 9 mostly doing meetings if I'm not traveling. All day and then I typically get home by early evening and work until after dinner with my family.

Christopher, a president of a private university, acknowledged that his wife's choice to commit to being a stay-at-home mother, even when she had a promising career ahead of her after graduate school, has contributed to his ability to have such a time-consuming leadership role.

[…] she chose, when we had kids, to stay home and sometimes she struggles with that a little bit, some

of her friends don't sort of respect that decision the way – I guess they don't appreciate that she made it in freedom. You know. I certainly encouraged her to do whatever she wanted to do if she wanted to stay home; we'll make that work on one income. If she wants to work, we'll make that work somehow. Whatever she wanted and she was the one who said – I think that we've succeeded when women can make that choice as I said sort of in total freedom and they won't feel insignificant if they stay home or if they work or whatever. We're not quite there yet but hopefully, we're making progress. She elected to do that. Fortunately, we could afford to do that and you know I guess the big question is maybe I should have thought about staying home at some point and she could have. And, I think if I had done that, I would have been doing it to prove a point, not because it's what I wanted to do. So, let's get to a point where people do what they want to do not what they feel society allows them to do or forces them to do. So, maybe there's a corollary there somehow.

Christopher's thoughts are insightful because he acknowledges that his success as an administrator is largely due to his wife's promise to keep household affairs in order while he was off doing his job. Furthermore, he recognized the gendered imbalance here in which it is more common for women to forgo their professional careers for family, than it is for men to do the same.

Frederick expressed how he sensed a gendered imbalance with regard to work and family obligations when he picked up his children from daycare while his wife was at her part-time job.

> *I'd show up at this very kind of enclosed [space] and I'd be one of two men there amongst thirty or forty women waiting for their kids and how uncomfortable that was and how I felt they made me feel uncomfortable like you're in our space, what are you doing here? Go get a job. Why aren't you at work? And, from that experience, I realized what women must feel like in many of these situations where they come into the room and they're counting. They're saying there are two women in here and there are eight guys; this is going to be bad news.*

While Frederick addressed his experience with a gendered assumption that it was a woman's job to pick up children from daycare, Douglas, a president at a public university, acknowledged that he has benefited from living alone for the majority of the academic year. Douglas addressed the career benefits associated with his long-distance, commuter relationship with his wife during the academic year, who is a faculty member elsewhere. This structure has given him even more flexibility as a president to be present at even more meetings and events than his job entails.

> *We are used to this lifestyle but it's really helped me in the presidency because during the week, when – how many basketball games can I watch on ESPN? So, I'm really available to go to student events or be on campus and so forth.*

Frederick, Douglas, Paul, and Christopher each talked about family-related matters in relation to the work and family balance and the way in which their individual families chose to manage it. Women and men leaders drew a connection between their work and family balance and the factors that alleviated the burden. Women reported negotiating for closer living arrangements as I noted earlier with Joanne's experience, postponing leadership, and prioritizing family over work. Men expressed gratitude toward their supportive wives, contributed when possible and convenient, and noted how a separate living arrangement could create an ideal professional environment. Christopher acknowledged that societal expectations of suitable work for men kept him from ever seriously considering life as a stay-at-home father. As such, while women were more likely to make life-changing decisions based on the needs of their families, men were also quite aware of the implications that their roles had for their families.

GENDER AND POWER

Analysis of my respondents' insights reveals the salient relationship between gender and power. This gendered dynamic became apparent through a questioning of authority, "power trips," sexual harassment, and other gender-based advantages.

QUESTIONING OF AUTHORITY

At work, we find that women are often held to different socially constructed standards than men; these differential standards often prevent women from rising to leadership positions. Women face a "double bind" (Lakoff, 1975) that poses a Catch-22 situation: women leaders who act in ways that are not socially expected of women and who do not take the emotions of others into account in their decisions may be labeled as "bitches;" women who are overly empathetic in their decision-making may be viewed as "pushovers."

In contrast, men who exhibit similar traits are more likely to be defined in more positive terms such as "decisive" and "considerate" leaders (Jamieson, 1995; Pini, 2005). This circumstance is limiting and disruptive for women at all levels of an employment hierarchy who face "gender trials" for transgressing gender norms (Pierce, 1995). These transgressions, in addition to other structural factors, may impose impediments to women's advancement. Women who are in positions of authority challenge historical traditions of patriarchy where men are responsible for institutional changes. Yet, my data analysis does not confirm that women disproportionately felt that institutional stakeholders questioned their authority. Both women and men reported numerous accounts in which others had challenged their responses to university matters. While it is difficult to know whether or not gender is responsible for any of the challenges, it is clear that both women and men higher educational leaders confronted intense scrutiny for their executive decisions.

Sabrina, the president of a public university, noted that people often questioned her authority. Her particular institution has an established culture of shared governance and openness in decision-making processes. Yet, Sabrina did speak of how she manages particular instances in which she feels as though she needs to command respect when others query her responses.

> *Yes, [laughs]. ... people question my authority all the time. Some people do it gently and some people do it more forcefully. And, sometimes I have to really – you know, make a decision. I mean, think it through, make a decision and stick to my guns. No matter what, people are questioning my authority. If I feel that I am doing the right thing for [name of institution] and for the students then I stick to*

*my guns no matter who questions my authority.
But, yes it's questioned all the time because people,
people believe sometimes that you shouldn't be
making that decision, that you should be sharing
the decision making. And, there are some cases
where it's not to be shared, it's a presidential matter
and a president decides.*

Sabrina described an instance in which she held on to the reins of her presidential authority while faced with heated faculty disapproval over a course schedule change. She reminded faculty of her responsibility for budgetary matters and her overall concern with graduation rates that superseded faculty interests in course timing. By defending and explaining her position, she held onto her influence.

Corinne, a provost at a private university, noted similar faculty disapproval with regard to budgetary and curriculum changes that she had proposed and describes how she addressed the contention:

*It's about somebody else being angry because
they feel their program is being devalued in your
eyes and to sort of separate that professional and
personal piece. So, you know, a lot of times you get
the comment or somebody decides that it's their
time to get on the bully pulpit. You're standing in
front of the faculty senate and there's nowhere to
go. You have to stand there and take it. It's just
to try to be kind of neutral and to sort of listen as
respectfully as possible and then take a pause and
again not to respond quickly and to know that your
buttons can be pushed. […] Even if the response
is – "I'm sorry we have to, respectfully, I just can't
agree with you."*

In this instance, Corinne held to her conviction by doing what she felt was best for the university. She listened to dissatisfactions with the proposed changes; however, she acted in what she deemed to be the best interest of the university.

Eugene, a dean at a public university also spoke of instances in which faculty had questioned his authority:

> *Oh yes, it happens many times. There are instances when it is very severe and it is nasty to some extent and there are cases when people say, "I don't agree with you. I don't accept it, but I take it." [...] Mild instances here – in this place – but, severe cases at least in two other places – severe cases. And, one of the cases was another male who just – you know – I don't want to make a judgment whether I was right or this person was right – but, just had this habit of not wanting to basically be cooperative and cooperate and then I was also challenged and not dealt with professional courtesy and respect needed when I was dean actually by a female faculty who had grievances [...] I had a couple working in the same department, in the same field. And, in that system – we had these merit pay increases. It was a little amount of money; it wasn't huge. But, in order to be objective, my staff and other deans – we came up with a formula. We said, we can't be subjective, we can't say, I like this person – I don't like. Let's do the formula and put everything in there and then based on that – we'll say – you get $500, you get a thousand, you get 200 and the amount of money to be divided wasn't huge, it was very small. And, it happened that somehow the score of the husband was higher and got a couple of hundred dollars more than the wife. And, the wife was upset and*

> *took it as a gender bias [...] she never forgave me for that.*

Eugene remained calm and confident in his decision to implement a transparent and objective policy. Eugene dealt with intense disapproval that subsequently lingered for years.

Similar to Eugene, Jake reported that faculty had questioned his authority to such an extent that he had to overtake a hiring matter. Jake was forced to intervene and say that if the department did not make the hire, he would do it himself:

> *This year the [discipline name] department asked for a visitor, we gave them a visitor – we said, it's going to be on a 3/2 schedule and they then decided not to hire that visitor. And, I had to tell them, "Look, the students need those classes. If you don't hire the visitor, I'm going to hire the visitor." And, actually this week they are reconsidering the policy – but, we'll see.*

Jake acted in the best interest of the students and the university in making his decision and he stood his ground in the face of this disapproval.

Yet, Steven, the provost of a public university, indicated that when others question his authority, he sees it as an opportunity for dialogue and for further examination of his motivations for coming to such a decision:

> *Well, they [the stakeholders] would question for example why we make certain decisions and many times I feel that they have every right to ask. We are a public university that needs to be transparent but they may not understand the full scope, the entire story. So, I do share the reasons, the constraints and the thought process that resulted*

> *in my making the decision. Now, at the end of that process my reasoning could have been flawed or my assumptions could have been flawed and if there's a better way, I'll go back and revisit it. So, I know that some leaders once they lay down their mandate, they need to or they feel the need to maintain their reputation as being decisive so that they do not like to reverse their decision. But, for me, if there's a better way to arrive at a solution, we'll get there.*

Steven's reaction to this disapproval demonstrates his openness toward process-based decision-making. Sometimes, decisions may seem exceptionally obvious for leaders. Yet, other times when formulating new policies, it is advisable to reflect on a decision before implementing a policy with significant opposition. Furthermore, it is important to implement a level of transparency in decision-making to temper the questioning of authority.

Similarly, Marcus, the Provost at a public university, talked about how he has learned to deal with others questioning his authority through openness and respect for his peers.

> *I would describe it [the questioning of authority] on a couple of levels. One is the kind of discussion that happens in a private office environment. Anyone is free to disagree about whatever they want to disagree about on a certain policy or guideline. But, in order for an institution to have integrity and consistency, once that discussion is done and either the President or myself has made a recommendation, then that's what it has to be. So, if that person leaves my office and then goes around campus saying well, I tried to convince the Provost,*

> *but he just wouldn't agree and then they're really angry and then they go around trying to undermine the discussion, that does damage, so you end up going backwards.*

Emily, the provost at a public university, mirrored Steven and Marcus' experiences when others have questioned their authority. Emily described how she has developed an appreciation for transparency and the dialogue that ensues from disapproval:

> *I'm willing to share authority and power as much as possible. I think if I give somebody else the right to make a decision, that doesn't mean that I have less power or less authority. I think in most cases it just means that I realize that that person is going to do something better or make a better decision and should have the right to do so. So, I don't have a problem with that. So, I would say it's often questioned but you know, it's not in a way that's ever been a problem, I don't think. And, sometimes I will just say to people, that's my job and I'm the one to make the decision and that's the decision that I made and I'll live with the consequences.*

Nadine, the president of a private liberal arts college, noted that she also faces others who question her authority on a regular basis and expressed how she handles such situations via respect:

> *And, it's kind of one of those things where authority; you have anyone in an administrative role, you do know what your authority is and there are rules and regulations that people follow and so if you violate some type of rule, sexual harassment, something like that – there's no flexibility. This is*

> *the way it works and this is it. On the other hand, I think leaders – they do have authority. But, by and large, more gets by if you have the trust and the good will of a community.*

Having stakeholder buy-in on a decision, when possible, is particularly important. Of course, everyone is not going to agree on every decision that an administrator makes; however, an institution will function much more smoothly if stakeholders feel that their opinions are valued and that they are not blindly following authority. Ronald, a president of a public university, talked about the importance of having buy-in from his direct reports and his belief that wielding his authority to tell someone how to solve a problem was not a viable way of approaching his work. As such, he welcomed a questioning of his authority given that it meant that the person implementing a policy believed in the problem-solving process:

> *What I value in people that report to me, leaders but in my relationship with them is – and I tell them all this on numerous occasions, I say look – you need to be – you won't be comfortable in this job if you're not comfortable with me asking you a bunch of questions. When we're done – 99.99% of the time we're going to do it your way. But, you have to be okay with me going wait a minute. Why on Earth do you think we should do this? To me, that seems crazy. Tell me; give me two reasons why we should do X instead of Y. And I said, even if you don't convince me. As long as you believe in it and you got a decent idea. We're going to do it your way, even if I don't think it's the best way. Why? Because you will do better with a bad idea that you believe in than with my good idea that you hate.*

Heavy-handed responses in which an administrator responds to others' questioning with ultimatums that do not allow for open dialogue are uncharacteristic of university leadership. Women and men as leaders confront challenges to their decisions and I did not identify any gendered differences in how they chose to deal with that contention. Furthermore, I did not get an overwhelming sense that respondents felt that women leaders faced more challenges than men leaders did. For example, Caroline, a president at a public university did acknowledge that she had faced more questioning prior to becoming president that may have been rooted in gendered assumptions. When I asked Caroline if anyone had ever questioned her presidential authority, she noted:

> *Nobody, I mean that's one of the only truly great things about being a president is no one questions your authority. Now, that's not true for every other job I've had where even if it's the area where you do have authority, people question you. Women probably get that more than men do but yeah – when you're finally the president that finally stops. I mean – they may hate your decision, they may think you're an idiot, but they don't question your authority. When you're the provost, when you're the dean, when you're the chair, people are always questioning your authority. They are always trying to go over your head. Like for me, there's nobody to go over my head to. They can go to the – people tend not to go to the Board of Trustees most places because I think they know that the trustees work with the president. The President is basically on the Board, so the buck does stop here.*

For Caroline, she credits the questioning of authority more to her positional standing than she equates it to her gender.

As it turned out, age and the amount of time that respondents had held a position was a salient factor in managing questions of authority. Anna, a provost at a public university, and Douglas, a president at a public university, had reported that earlier on in their careers, they had faced more questioning. Furthermore, Christopher, a fairly new president of a private university of just about a year, reported recent power struggles over a particular budget and faculty compensation issue. As such, age, experience, or tenure on the job, and the hierarchal level of a leader's position may contribute more to the likelihood of the questioning of authority in higher educational leadership, than gender. How do women and men exercise their power as administrators? Are women and men equally as likely to abuse their power through arrogant displays of authority?

"POWER TRIPS"

When I asked respondents to consider examples of ineffective leadership, it was common for them to recount witnessing leaders who had demonstrated extreme manifestations of their authority. My respondents reported that both women and men were capable of engaging in such "power trips" in which they visibly displayed their command over others. Yet, it was interesting to find that in instances pertaining to women, it was often equated to gender and a woman's need to prove her worth in a male-dominated environment. On the other hand, when respondents reported that men had shown such outward and domineering behavior, gender was not identified as a variable. Ronald, the president of a public university, talked about his observations of women in administrative roles that exhibited outward authoritarian actions:

> *[...] not that there aren't men with these traits. But, I think they may be a bit more common in women. I've known women who really were very retiring type individuals and they know it and so their response is to act extra tough and start tipping over tables to show people who's the boss. It doesn't work. It aggravates people; it irritates people. But they feel like if they don't do that as a woman, at least I think – I mean, I'm not a woman so I don't. But, I think that they feel like well people won't take me seriously. People won't – if it was a guy – oh yeah, he could do this. [...] But, as a woman, if I don't show them that by God, I'll get right in your face if I have to – and they're a little more reticent to just kind of let the game come to them a little bit and take it a little bit easy and say, "Hey, I'm a nice person," which is really more important to people, I think then – as long as you're competent – I think being a nice person is probably more important.*

Ronald finds that it is more important for women and men to be amenable as leaders than it is to outwardly demonstrate authority.

Bradford, a dean at a private university, addressed differences in women and men's leadership with regard to observations that he has had regarding some women's assertiveness. Bradford equates this "pushiness" to an inherited male model of leadership that is currently an outdated and ineffective mode of leadership.

> *I work with an associate dean who's a woman ... my provost is a woman. My last provost was a woman. And in those cases, I can't really psychoanalyze the present provost at all. I don't know where her*

style comes from. But, the other two are in what you might consider, you can help me with this, you might consider this "old school." But, their position is, it doesn't matter whether you're a woman or not, just lead and get it done and I see that as somewhat "old school."

He continued to describe common scenarios involving these women and their leadership style:

It's like they're putting blinders on to the gender aspect. They are successful, but I don't know why. Sometimes I think they can be a little bit, logic tells me that this is the answer, therefore, I will do it. And, whereas, it's kind of a paradox. I have a male associate dean that will go, [Bradford] this will make 8 people angry, here are their names. So, the woman is the one going – just push it through – and I think that that may be a sense of having affiliated to male models of leadership early on.

In Chapter 3, I noted the example from Samuel, a dean at a private liberal arts college, who talked about a previous president who had overextended her authority and who chose to use her power in circumstances when her influence was not warranted. Subsequently, that president came off as "pushy" and "gratuitous."

Jake, the provost at a private university, did not specifically comment on an example of a leader who had demonstrated an overtly harsh demonstration of authority, he did acknowledge that as a man, his experience as provost is much different from a woman's experience as provost. As such, one can infer that a "power trip" would be less likely in such a circumstance given that he already has the respect of the community. When I asked if he could recall a situation in which he felt that he was treated less for being a provost and more because of his gender, he stated:

> *So, this is really a question – it seems to be more for women than for men. At some time that I cease to become provost because I was just a woman. I mean – because I'm already the dominant gender, I don't really have that problem too much. No one ever says to me – because you're a man, I'm not going to pay any attention to you being the provost. I mean they pay attention to me for both reasons, unfortunately.*

During my interview with Jake, he actually referred to his leadership style as maternal and found that this is more suitable to an academic environment where hierarchies with little room for open discussion are disadvantageous. As such, based on this observation, one might argue that it may be easier for a man to exhibit a maternal style of leadership given that he has a strong foundation of support, based on his dominant gender, from the onset (and for that to be seen as an asset rather than unprofessional).

It was not as common to find that my women respondents equated gender with power when it came to women or men leaders; however, Cynthia, a dean at a private liberal arts college, and Lisa, a dean at a private university, each spoke of instances in which they felt as though men who were their superiors wielded their authority over them. I spoke about Cynthia's interactions with her provost, who was a man, earlier in this chapter. Lisa spoke about an earlier time in her career when, as the first tenure-track woman in the department, she confronted an overwhelming power battle with more senior departmental colleagues:

> *I was doing things differently. So, I could have been a man in the department doing things*

> *differently. And, it would be okay. But, what I was doing differently, it wasn't safe. They didn't see it as the safe path. So, each of the things I've done has been unconventional. And, didn't recognize it as being either really challenging, to reward it or would try to pull me back and say you're doing the wrong thing, you need to do that thing. So, I think between that and senior faculty in the department who used power in an inappropriate way, there were just inequities all over the place.*

Cynthia and Lisa observed men's power trips. Caroline's commentary with regard to unequal judgment of women's leadership captures the inequality that women may confront regarding their decisions. I am not implying that women cannot be pushier than men can be for reasons beyond gendered understandings; however, I believe that Caroline's observation depicts women's challenges in expressing their influence, especially earlier on in their careers:

> *I've sometimes talked to women's groups and ACE leadership workshops and women and I've told all of them – if you want to go into leadership, people will call you a bitch – they are calling you a bitch right now. Any time you make a hard decision – they are saying – and you've got to be comfortable with that. I mean, you've got to think – people out there are calling me a bitch and I don't care. [...] I used to have meetings sometimes where I gave people – you know I was mad and then later I was like – was I too harsh? And, so you get a – you know, I don't do it a lot anymore – and then you stop doing it, but, you're doing it for a long time. And, you have got to let go of that. But, people are*

> *calling you a bitch or worse behind your back if you're a strong leader, if you're making decisions. And, you've got to be comfortable with that. [...] Maybe, twenty years from now or thirty years from now – it will be degendered.*

Caroline's insights mirror the Catch-22 dynamic that women face for making decisions that may appear to be too harsh (Jamieson, 1995; Pini, 2005). Everyone is capable of misusing power in such a way that we would call these misappropriations, or "power trips." Yet, it is important to note that given the relative novelty of women's leadership in our society, women's power trips may sometimes be characterized through a lens that is not accustomed to seeing women in these positions. Furthermore, in some cases, women may resort to extreme manifestations of power because of a long history of not being taken seriously. Sexual harassment is one prime example of women's gendered experiences with men's unsolicited power.

WORKPLACE HARASSMENT

Gender-based harassment, particularly sexual harassment (Chamberlain, Crowley, Tope, & Hodson, 2008; McLaughlin, Uggen, & Blackstone, 2012; Zippel, 2006) can pollute a work environment and severely affect workplace affairs. Over time, a woman who has confronted a reproachful workplace environment develops strategies for balancing that negativity. In a few instances, respondents indicated that they had witnessed or experienced workplace gender-based harassment and described how they overcame this harassment.

Anna, a provost at a public university, noted that earlier on in her career, she had experienced sexual harassment.

Although Anna did not label these experiences as sexual harassment, based on the unwarranted sexual attention that disrupted the workplace, I am referring to these incidents as sexual harassment. I asked Anna to comment on whether or not she had ever felt that she was treated less for being a provost and more because of her gender. She instantly responded: "No. Not anymore." But she did describe such experiences in the past:

> *Oh yeah. Thirty years ago, yeah, 20 years ago yeah. [...] These issues – gender issues have been hugely a part of my life, but they were more of an issue when I was young and attractive than they are. And, I'm not saying I'm unattractive – but, you know, once you get to be 60, the games that people play are not games any more. You just learn to not deal with them. So, I simply don't deal with them. I don't have to any more.*

Anna noted the relevance of age as a diminishing factor in a woman's experience and developed coping mechanisms with regard to sexual harassment in the workplace.[1]

> *[...] when I was young and people flirted with me – or when I was young and there were sexual innuendos or there were things that were said that were ridiculous – I find – as you reach a certain age that nonsense stops. You don't have to – the interesting thing would be to be 30 in 2013 as opposed to 30 in 1980 and to have had the opportunities to see how it is for women today when I was younger because I can't answer that question for younger women today. But, there's a certain point in your life when you just become comfortable with who you are and you grow*

> *into leadership roles and you're not afraid to be a leader. And, you're not afraid to make a decision. There's also the time when you stop worrying about everybody liking you and just understanding that you should always do the right thing and that respect is way more important than being liked. When you're younger, especially when you're a young woman, I think a lot of young women leaders and administrators get caught up in worrying about – will people like them. And, there's a certain point where you – at least in my career and I think in some of my colleagues who are females' career – you don't worry about that anymore. You just try to do the right thing.*

Likewise, Corrine, a provost at a private university, also noted the age factor and the transition she underwent in developing coping mechanisms for withstanding gender-based harassment:

> *There have been periods when I've been more aware of my gender than I am currently. I'm older now. I don't take shit from anybody. When I was your age [meaning in one's thirties], and somebody made a comment about appearance that felt inappropriate or if I were going into a meeting I would kind of wonder am I signaling something through my dress? And, again the work that I've done with women, am I diminishing my size, do I need to take more space because I was quite petite when I was younger. And that can be a problem especially if you're petite and you look young. […] I was much more aware about how I said what I said, how I portrayed myself physically as a woman*

> *when I was younger. Right now, take it or leave. I
> don't take any shit from anybody. And, I've earned it.*

When asked to consider whether or not age was a salient factor for men's experiences in the workplace and if she feels that it is also relevant for men. Corrine acknowledged:

> *I do. I think men get there too. I still think though
> for women it's still a little different. [...] You really
> get to a point where you think there is a wisdom
> that one just assumes. And, I think men in a room
> will grant me that because I have grey hair now.
> Where they wouldn't have if I would have entered
> the room twenty years ago or thirty years ago.*

Caroline, a president of a public university, also reported experiencing workplace harassment in the past. Yet, for Caroline, it was in the more recent past. Here, she talks about her experience with a "bully boss:"

> *It was my last job where it was really a horrendous
> boss, abusive. And, it was highly gendered and
> everything and then I was pretty senior, like I had
> my own relationship with the Board. So, I wasn't
> afraid like people are who are lower down.*

Yet, in terms of her present-day struggles, Caroline did not mention harassment as an issue that she either witnessed or experienced. Caroline also acknowledged that she was not certain if she could tie this past mistreatment to gender, or if it was related to other factors such as a difference in disciplinary background. Again, similar to Anna and Corrine, this harassment took place in the past. Now that she has an even more respected executive role, she is beyond the realm of such mistreatment. Caroline did not particularly talk about age or experience as contributing factors for past mistreatment. However, it is clear that she, like Anna and Corinne, faced workplace obstacles that one may either partially or exclusively attribute to gender and power dynamics.

In two different, but related instances, Matthew, a dean at a private university, and Douglas, a president at a public university, reported women's gendered reactions to women assuming positions of authority on their campuses. In these instances, the questioning was based on dress and allegiance to feminist issues in addition to potential assertiveness. Matthew noted rumored behind-the-scenes chatter and disparaging comments from women regarding a hiring decision for the university's new provost:

> *When the one person whose name was being floated and was the front runner and did indeed get it, there was some strange negativity that came up toward her and it came up in these anecdotes only from women of a senior, almost the first generation of tenured women and now this woman is more feminine, not more feminine – she wears dresses more, she's more style conscious – that I could easily say and some of the discussion had to be about her sense of solidarity in the past with women's issues. She actually studies women's issues, but not on campus. She wasn't a player in the women's caucus or something like that from an earlier period.*

Here, it is apparent how women can also wield gender-based harassment toward other women. Matthew noted the inappropriateness regarding an individual's dress and the ability to do a job well.

Furthermore, Douglas reported a past situation at a previous university in which the new president, who was a woman, asked him to recommend someone for the job of provost.[2] When he recommended a woman for the provost job with whom the new president was not familiar, he was surprised by the president's response:

> *I said our dean [of a particular college] was a really good person. And, I think she has credibility. And, she said, "Is she tough enough? And, it was wrong to ask that question. And, she hired someone else who was tough and they both lasted two years. Votes of no confidence, they were gone.*

Here, it is apparent how sexual harassment and gender-based harassment can take place with regard to a hiring decision and that women can also be responsible for inflicting this offensive power.

All of the examples in this section depict gendered situations in which others made offhand comments that created a potentially harmful work environment for the respondents and the individuals who were being considered for advancement. The majority of the examples in this chapter have referred to women's experience with a weakening of power with regard to traditional gender roles, the work and family balance, questioning of authority, and unwarranted gendered power dynamics. How might women experience gendered advantages with regard to their power within the leadership hierarchy?

GENDERED ADVANTAGES: IS THE GLASS CEILING BROKEN?

Often, women can advance only so far before they hit a glass ceiling that they cannot break due to a lack of mentoring

(Kantola, 2008; Lorber, 1984) or sexist perceptions about women's ability to lead given an absence of prior women in leadership positions (Archer, 2013; Schull, Shaw, & Kihl, 2013; Williams, 1992, 1995). This glass ceiling that women will inevitably confront in some manifestation at both lower-level and higher-level management positions (Britton & Williams, 2000; Ferree & Purkayastha, 2000), and men's ability to ride a "glass escalator"[3] in all workplaces regardless of the work responsibilities that may traditionally be associated with men or women (Williams, 1992, 1995), reveals structural gendered inequality in the workplace.

Valian (2004) reported that difficulties that women face in advancing to academic leadership positions are rooted in gender schemas that influence how society disadvantages and under-evaluates women. While women have historically faced challenges within their trajectory on the leadership hierarchy, particularly in STEM fields and administration (Bird, 2011; Bystydzienski & Bird, 2006; Xie & Shauman, 2003), some of my respondents reported that women might face gender-based advantages in their leadership ascendancy. Having women in key university leadership positions sends the message to other marginalized groups, particularly among the student population, that opportunities exist for them. An institution establishes a reputation for itself that subsequently improves its future (Valian, 2004). Having women in positions of authority sends a message that an institution is forward thinking, progressive, and prepared for path-breaking innovations. We still live in an era in which witnessing first women presidents at universities is common. While some respondents recognized that women have historically faced (and some continue to face) gendered disadvantages in the workplace, they acknowledged that women's gender identity could also serve an enabling role toward leadership advancement.

For example, Isabella, a provost at a public university, framed her thoughts on gender and leadership with regard to the legacy of male-dominated leadership positions that had previously been the standard at this university that presently has a woman serving as president. She finds that the climate has completely reversed. Isabella's response implies that women may now face advantages as a result of not continuing a tradition that had been marked by a lack of transparency.

> *So, mostly I've heard that the reflection on the previous administration as a bunch of good ol' boys. I haven't heard the reflection on [the current president's] actions as a result of being a woman. It's more, it's almost as if people are saying we finally got some balance here because there was a lot of smoke-filled room decision making, lack of transparency. Now, it's not that I don't think that there are gender biases. I mean, sure I see them in meetings or whatever. [...] But, there are groups of colleagues on this campus where I notice stronger biases against women and I know that women on this campus have those experiences and I believe them to be real. I don't think they're making it up; it just hasn't been a part of my experience. But, I think the reflection that I've heard is more often than not a comment about behavior that people found distasteful previously rather than imbuing the current decision making with this gender identity.*

While Isabella cannot claim that differences in the previous leadership were gender based, the absence of the "good ol' boys" network has had its benefits for the institution.

Earlier in this chapter, I noted that Caroline, the president at a public university, had identified gender-based discrimination and stakeholders' gender-based responses to her decisions. On the other hand, Caroline noted that there are times in which women may face advantages that are gender based:

> *[...] sometimes people liked it [the fact that she is a woman] like I had an advantage being female because they think it's new, it's different. So, I probably got more opportunities.*

While Joanne, the provost at a private liberal arts college, did not acknowledge that being a woman had helped her to advance to her present role, she did acknowledge an emphasis on gender-based mentoring. She noted the past practices of her present institution that helped women make the transition from assistant to associate professors:

> *One of the things we used to do at [her present institution] was pair female faculty assistant professors with tenured faculty and so I think that was part of the culture here for a while.*

Men who have traditionally held senior academic positions for years have also benefited from formal and informal mentoring practices. As such, Joanne's insight denotes the benefit that women may have when entering new assistant professor positions given that there is a significant push today to see women succeed. Furthermore, my earlier discussion of gender-specific leadership trainings establishes a basis for claiming that women may also be at an advantage because supervisors may be more likely to direct them to such trainings given that they are so widely discussed and noted in academic circles. Women may then disproportionately benefit from this focused, gender-specific training that allows them to form camaraderie with other women leaders spanning a variety of institutions.

While I did not get an overwhelming sense from my interviews that any of the men respondents felt that they had been disadvantaged as a result of women's achievements, Samuel, a dean at a private liberal arts college, indicated that he had felt that his gender had worked against him. Samuel discussed the oppositional exchange that occurred between him and his predecessor who was a woman:

> *[Name of his predecessor] did not think I should be the dean. And, we'll get to one of these lovely gendered things here. I had been the associate dean for four years. [Name of predecessor] gave me glowing reviews and to this day if you ask her, "Did [Samuel] do a good job?" She will tell you I did a fantastic job as associate dean. [...] But, she was of the opinion that the college especially since the president at the time was male needed to have a woman in this office and she felt enough that way that she would not recommend me for the job and said, I'm just going to keep my own counsel on that. And, she and I had long conversations about that. I thought it was really despicable of her. But, okay, one of the other things about [name of his predecessor] that I really admire although I don't try to emulate this is she was a woman who has principles that trump everything else. I think pragmatism ought to sometimes trump principle. But, we can talk about what are the limits of that. But, her principle was that if the president were male, they would absolutely need to have a woman [as dean]. So, when I took over it was sort of "here's the keys; don't drive it into a ditch."*

While I did not encounter similar observations from other participants, it is possible that such a dynamic may characterize future discussions on college campuses regarding the gendered chain of command. It is still premature to say that women have broken the glass ceiling in academia. Yet, the insights from my respondents reveal a friendlier climate for women in academic leadership.

Gender undoubtedly influences university administrators' leadership experiences. Yet, as institutions become accustomed to having women in leadership roles, we are seeing a mitigation of women's gendered experiences that negatively affect their work. Regardless of women's personal experiences with gender-based responses to their leadership, it is apparent that we have not yet arrived at a situation in which women are free from being labeled as "queens" or "bitches" as they carry out their work. Over time, women in leadership roles may also become either immune from or desensitized to gender-disparaging comments. As some respondents observed, women may in fact have benefitted from an emphasis on ridding universities of the "good ol' boys" networks that once ran the show through greater attention to women's professional development.

The intimate stories that administrators shared demonstrate that gender still figures prominently into academic leaders' narratives. We must be aware of the significance that gender plays at all levels of an academic leadership hierarchy. All leaders experience gender in very meaningful ways whether or not it is through their own experiences or their interpretation of others' experiences. The promise of degendering leadership (Lorber, 1994, 2000, 2005) and opening up opportunities for non-cisgender leaders can only be achieved through this ongoing focus. Attention to and an emphasis on deteriorating the labeling of leadership as "feminine" or "masculine" is part of this endeavor.

NOTES

1. Haraway's (1991) concept of the cyborg, which has superhuman tendencies: who is "almost mechanically perfect – made to perfection by a male-dominated world" (Muhr, 2011, p. 338) clarifies this phenomenon in which a woman can come to tolerate disparaging gendered comments, for example. Muhr (2011) notes that the success of the cyborgian leader is based on her astute balancing act of masculinity and femininity that confines her in an inescapable "gendered machine" (p. 354).

2. Douglas had announced his departure and he noted that he felt that the president would have made him provost had he not been on his way out.

3. The glass escalator concept maintains that in work institutions where women are the majority, men receive preferential treatment by supervisors and peers. This exceptionally positive and welcoming treatment may facilitate men's promotion and advancement in fields such as nursing where women are commonly in the majority. In such instances, a novice man, whose expertise and training mirrors that of a veteran woman employee, will be swiftly promoted to the role of overseer because of the stereotypical understanding that men are meant to be leaders. As such, men ride an escalator to the top of a work hierarchy as a result of archetypal pairings of men with leadership.

5

CONCLUSION, IMPLICATIONS, AND SUGGESTIONS

Even if we all [the women presidents] got together and tried to work on this [degendering leadership], I don't think we could. There's not enough of us and we're too different – styles and all that. So, some of it I think is probably just a matter of time [...].
Caroline, president at a public university

It is possible to define academic leadership without relying on gendered socially constructed definitions, rooted in traditional gender roles. While gender is certainly relevant to an academic leader's career path and experience navigating the leadership hierarchy, women and men's leadership styles in academia are more similar than they are different.

Respondents' accounts of personal leadership challenges constructed their understandings of how gendered frameworks may work in the backdrop of leaders' workplace interactions. Collectively, the narratives create a broad definition of academic leadership that is absent of gender, race, class, ethnicity, sexuality, or age. Multiple factors contribute to a leader's efficacy, one of which is the ability to adapt to new situations by listening to stakeholders and learning from the mistakes of others. Effective academic leadership is not feminine or masculine; it encompasses understanding the institutional culture, respecting the position, and prioritizing the interests of stakeholders through shared governance and transparent decision-making. These standards are not gendered; they are universal and displace the problematic feminine and masculine leadership divide.

Academic leaders' insights on early pathways did not reveal gendered differences regarding modeling or not modeling others' behavior, learning on the job, or listening to stakeholders. Faculty mentoring and encouragement from faculty advisors at early stages in a leader's career contributed to leaders' realization that a career in academia was right for them and that they should focus on scholarship. As faculty, respondents noted the importance of leaders' recognition of their leadership potential. Modeling best practices of mentors in addition to figureheads with whom respondents did not have personal relations also proved to be relevant for respondents who sought strength from their counterparts. On the other hand, learning from others' failings was often just as important as learning from their successes. This openness and "on-the-job" learning through listening and action proved to be exceptionally noteworthy for these leaders who care for their institutions and want to ensure their viability. These aforementioned experiences, that did not present any noteworthy gendered differences, suggest an absence of a gendered framework in the refinement of leadership skills.

Yet, gender-based differences are distinct when an already-accomplished woman is priming herself for further advancement. At this time, she may turn to, or she may be encouraged to attend gender-specific leadership trainings that are a response to women's historical marginalization from leadership positions. These trainings provide an opportunity for

Conclusion, Implications, and Suggestions

women to network within a gender-specific context in which they can share insights on coping strategies for gender-based inequalities that they may have encountered in the workplace with regard to harassment, the work and family balance, or gender roles. As women advance to academic leadership positions in larger numbers, we may find more hesitancy than I uncovered with regard to these separate trainings that imply men's natural command of leadership and women's need for further training. Trainings can be exceptionally helpful for all, especially those with limited prior leadership training. Building networks through non-gender-specific academic leadership trainings effectively aims to overcome an "old boys' network" and encourages leadership degendering. Furthermore, programing for all historically marginalized populations has its benefits, as long as it is not characterizing and generalizing leadership from these groups as fundamentally different. The same premise holds true as with gender; social position shapes experiences, but traits, such as our capacity to lead, are not fundamentally different because of our social location.

Women's historical absence from positions of higher educational leadership contributed to their ability to acknowledge the role that gender played in their career trajectories. While gender is a salient issue for both women and men in these administrative positions, women, more often than men, were able to identify moments in their career when they felt as though their gender had impacted a situation in a negative way. Furthermore, of the men respondents, while they could not significantly uncover similar personal experiences, they were incredibly perceptive toward women's gendered experiences that complicated the work structure. Traditional gender roles may pervade women's interactions with their peers leading others to question their resistance toward gendered power dynamics. While both women and men, particularly in labor-intensive employment requiring their constant attention, confront problems related to the work and family balance, women more often than men reported that they had postponed leadership until their children were older. Women were less likely to put their jobs over their families. As such, age became a salient factor here given that, as women's children were grown and they themselves were older, gender mattered less. Gender intersects with age in important ways; age is a source of power for women in leadership roles as others acknowledge the wisdom that comes with age and experience.

Other manifestations of gender and power that emerged from my data relate to a questioning of authority, excessive power displays, harassment, and women's gendered advantages. Colleges and universities are hotbeds for open deliberation and criticisms. Faculty members, in particular, are not shy about questioning new university initiatives if they are not in line with their personal vision. As such, women and men academic administrators face similar pressures from stakeholder questioning. It is simply a part of the academic culture for open dialogue to exist with regard to an institution's future direction. Often, respondents reported that women who publicly demonstrated heavy-handed decisions were trying to prove their worth within a traditionally male-dominated field. As such, overly domineering women face a gendered roadblock in the execution of tasks that men can surpass. This was one instance in which I identified a reproduction of gender stereotypes. Women are also more likely to be openly critiqued or demeaned based on gendered matters such as their dress, feminist commitment, and unwarranted sexual attention. These findings confirm how stakeholders can contribute to the gendering of leadership and represent how gender can create disadvantageous work environments for women.

My findings reveal the impossibility of gender blindness in academic leadership. While women and men's experiences often mirror one another, gender roles, assumptions about the work and family balance, and power dynamics that are rooted in traditional understandings of women's social roles characterize differential experiences for women and men. Yet, the reality of these socially constructed differences is that they do not suggest that women and men's leadership is fundamentally different. Women and men have different obstacles to face. At times, women respondents even reported feeling advantaged and men reported feeling disadvantaged as a result of institutional priorities to put women in office.

In sum, key takeaway messages of this book that can inform academia, that is often viewed as a space where progressive ideas can percolate and play out before their transmission to other institutions are as follows: (1) Gendering leadership is never constructive, even if it entails a positive focus on feminine leadership styles that make women more suitable to lead. (2) If we really want to continue to see an increase in leadership diversity, one that welcomes trans, nonbinary, and intersex leaders, we need to refrain from employing a trait gendering paradigm. (3) Stereotypes pertaining to race, sexuality, ethnicity, age, religion, and many other identities that sociologists study that can lead to leadership expectations associated with these respective identities are harmful and must be disentangled in this pursuit of leadership diversity. Leaders from different disciplines, racial and ethnic backgrounds, regions, institutional types, and administrative roles lead in very similar ways. The larger conversation here is that we need to systemically continue to develop an inclusive space for leadership diversity, so that colleges and universities can prepare future generations to be tolerant of all differences and skeptical of stereotypes that limit social progress.

SUGGESTIONS FOR FUTURE RESEARCH

The underrepresentation of respondents from historically marginalized backgrounds with respect to trans, non-binary, or intersex identity, race, class, sexuality, and ethnicity made it difficult for me to analyze my data through these lenses. Future research ought to look more closely at these variables to develop a more intersectional understanding of the degendering of leadership. To capture the nuances of leadership that supersede privileged, white, heterosexual, male paradigms of leadership, research ought to look at how trans, non-binary, and intersex identity, race, ethnicity, class, and sexuality contribute to defining leadership.

Lastly, future research might consider how university stakeholders degender leadership or reproduce gender stereotypes through their perceptions of academic leaders in visible leadership roles. My findings probe academic leaders for their responses on the gendering of leadership that are highly valuable given their public roles and path setting potential. Yet, insights from students, faculty members, staff members, alumni, the Board of Trustees, the community, and corporate and governmental partners regarding gender and leadership would allow for a different perspective and subsequently further enrichment of degendered leadership.

CONCLUSION

Most important to one of my initial research aims of envisioning degendered leadership, this study deconstructs the association of men and leadership and holds significance for existing theorizing on degendering. This analysis speaks about the fluidity and malleability of gender (Butler, 2004; Lorber, 1994, 2000, 2005) and offers an open-ended framework of leadership that is degendered and therefore the absence of gendered assumptions on how women or men ought to lead. Bromley (2013, p. 126) writes, "It is the gendered world itself that represents the problem [that women face in academia], not simply the exclusion of women or the existence of the male norm." Bromley (2013, p. 126) argues that we must strive "to make the academy gender-free." Envisioning a degendered leadership can be the starting point for degendering the academy.

INTERVIEW GUIDE

SECTION 1: BACKGROUND INFORMATION

(1) Can you talk about the path that you took that led you to your present leadership role at this institution? Please address how long you have held this role and your present responsibilities.

(2) What is your daily routine on the average workday?

(3) What do you perceive as the benefits and drawbacks to working in a higher educational administration setting as opposed to a corporate setting and as opposed to a governmental setting?

SECTION 2: DEFINING LEADERSHIP

(1) What is an example of effective leadership? How do you define leadership?

(2) Are certain people born to be leaders?

(3) What qualities does your institution value in its leaders?

(4) How does leadership shape your institution?

(5) Was there ever a time while serving in your present role where you were treated less for being a president, dean, or provost and more because of your gender?

SECTION 3: LEADERSHIP SKILLS

(1) Is there a particular leader that you admire that you may possibly look to as an example of the type of leader that you aspire to be in your work? Why?

(2) If you were to give advice to an aspiring leader who dreams of filling your shoes someday, what would that advice be?

(3) Have you ever taken part in a leadership workshop or seminar with regard to your present role (probe for background information, sponsorship, and attending population)? If yes, how useful were these workshops or seminars and who encouraged or sponsored you to attend this training?

(4) Do you lead trainings and orientations for university leaders on your campus? If yes, what are the core values that you stress in this programming? If no, does your institution not support these trainings?

(5) Do you take part in any informal mentoring groups on campus or off campus?

SECTION 4: LEADERSHIP CHALLENGES

(1) In your present role, have you ever encountered an ineffective leader?

(2) Do you maintain contact with other leaders in higher education administration (probe for age, race, gender, years of experience, and type of institution they came from)?

(3) Who mentored you? [Same probe as in Question 2.]

(4) Can you talk about a time when you might have faced a significant challenge in your present leadership role and how you addressed or resolved this challenge?

(5) Has anyone ever questioned your authority?

SECTION 5: CONCLUSION

(1) Is there anything else that you would like to address regarding your present leadership? Can you suggest another university leader who might be interested in taking part in my study? Would you feel comfortable introducing me to that individual via an e-mail introduction?

REFERENCES

Acker, J. (1990). Hierarchies, jobs, bodies: A theory of gendered organizations. *Gender & Society*, *4*(2), 139–158.

Acker, J. (1992). Gendering organizational theory. In A. J. Mills & P. Tancred (Eds.), *Gendering organizational analysis* (pp. 248–260). Newbury Park, CA: Sage Publications.

Acker, J. (2006). Inequality regimes: Gender, class, and race in organizations. *Gender & Society*, *20*(4), 441–464.

Agathangelou, A. M., & Ling, L. H. M. (2002). An unten(ur)able position: The politics of teaching for women of color in the US. *International Feminist Journal of Politics*, *4*(3), 368–398.

Alexander, M. J. (2005). *Pedagogies of crossing: Meditations on feminism, sexual politics, memory, and the sacred.* Durham, NC: Duke University Press.

Al-Lamky, A. (2007). Feminizing leadership in Arab societies: The perspectives of Omani female leaders. *Women in Management Review*, *22*(1), 49–67.

American Council on Education (ACE). (2017a). American College President Study 2017. Retrieved from https://www.acenet.edu/news-room/Pages/American-College-President-Study.aspx

American Council on Education (ACE). (2017b). Ready to lead: Women in the presidency. Retrieved from https://www.acenet.edu/news-room/Pages/Ready-to-Lead-Women-in-the-Presidency.aspx

American Council on Education (ACE). (2018). Women of color speak candidly about their path to the presidency. Retrieved from https://www.acenet.edu/news-room/Pages/Women-of-Color-Speak-Candidly-About-Their-Path-to-the-Presidency.aspx

Archer, E. M. (2013). The power of gendered stereotypes in the US marine corps. *Armed Forces & Society*, *39*(2), 359–391.

Bass, B. M. (1990). *Bass & Stodgill's handbook of leadership: Theory, research, and managerial applications* (3rd ed.). New York, NY: Free Press.

Bass, B. M. (1998). *Transformational leadership: Industrial, military, and educational impact*. Mahwah, NJ: Erlbaum.

Bird, S. (2011). Unsettling universities' incongruous, gendered bureaucratic structures: A case study approach. *Gender, Work, and Organization*, *18*(2), 202–230.

Birnbaum, R. (1992). *How academic leadership works: Understanding success and failure in the college presidency*. San Francisco, CA: Jossey-Bass:

Book, E. W. (2000). *Why the best man for the job is a woman*. New York, NY: HarperCollins.

Bowen, W. G., & Bok, D. (2000). *The shape of the river: Long-term consequences of considering race in college and university admissions*. Princeton, NJ: Princeton University Press.

Brescoll, V. L. (2011). Who takes the floor and why? Gender, power, and volubility in organizations. *Administrative Science Quarterly*, *56*(4), 622–641.

Britton, D. M. (1997). Gendered organizational logic: Policy and practice in men's and women's prisons. *Gender & Society, 11*(6), 796–818.

Britton, D. M. (2000). The epistemology of the gendered organization. *Gender & Society, 14*(3), 418–434.

Britton, D. M., & Williams, C. L. (2000). Response to Baxter and Wright. *Gender & Society, 14*(6), 804–808.

Bromley, L. (2013). The rules of the game: Women and the leaderist turn in higher education. *Gender and Education, 25*(1), 116–131.

Brown, H. (2009, October 6). Women college presidents' tough test. *Forbes.com*. Retrieved from http://www.forbes.com/2009/10/06/female-college-presidentsforbeswomanpowerwomen-tenure.html

Bruch, P. L., Jehangir, R. R., Lundell, D. B., Higbee, J. L., & Miksch, K. L. (2005). Communicating across differences: Toward a multicultural approach to institutional transformation. *Innovative Higher Education, 29*(3), 195–208.

Buchman, C., & DiPrete, T. A. (2006). The growing female advantage in college completion: The role of family background and academic achievement. *American Sociological Review, 71*(4), 515–541.

Budig, G. (2002). *A game of uncommon skill: Leading the modern college and university*. Westport, CT: Oryx Press.

Buller, J. (2011). *Academic leadership day by day: Small steps that lead to great success*. San Francisco, CA: Jossey-Bass.

Burns, J. M. (1978). *Leadership*. New York, NY: Harper & Row.

Butler, J. (1990). *Gender trouble: Feminism and the subversion of identity*. New York, NY: Routledge.

Butler, J. (2004). *Undoing gender*. London: Routledge.

Bystydzienski, J. M., & Bird, S. R. (2006). Introduction. In J. M. Bystydzienski & S. R. Bird (Eds.), *Removing barriers: Women in academic science, engineering, technology and mathematics careers* (pp. 1–19). Bloomington, IN: Indiana University Press.

Cann, A., & Siegfried, W. D. (1990). Gender stereotypes and dimensions of effective leadership behavior. *Sex Roles*, 23(7–8), 413–419.

Castro, M. R. (2012). Time demands and gender roles: The case of a big four firm in Mexico. *Gender, Work & Organization, 19*(5), 532–554.

Cha, Y. (2013). Overwork and the persistence of gender segregation in occupations. *Gender & Society*, 27(2), 158–184.

Chamberlain, L. J., Crowley, M., Tope, D., & Hodson, R. (2008). Sexual harassment in organizational context. *Work and Occupations*, 35(3), 262–296.

Chase, S. (1995). *Ambiguous empowerment: The work narratives of women school superintendents*. Amherst, MA: University of Massachusetts Press.

Cheung, F. M., & Halpern, D. F. (2010). Women at the top: Powerful leaders define success as work + family in a culture of gender. *American Psychologist*, 65(3), 182–193.

Chong, K. H. (2006). Negotiating patriarchy: South Korean Evangelical women and the politics of *gender*. *Gender & Society*, 20(6), 697–724.

Connell, R. (2006). The experience of gender in public sector organizations. *Gender, Work & Organization, 13*(5), 435–452.

Czarniawska, B. (2008). *A theory of organizing*. Cheltenham: Edward Elgar.

Damaske, S. (2011). *For the family?: How class and gender shape women's work*. New York, NY: Oxford University Press.

Davis, A. Y (2005). *Abolition democracy: Beyond empire, prisons, and torture*. New York, NY: Seven Stories Press.

Debebe, G. (2009). Transformational leadership in women's leadership development training. *Advancing Women in Leadership Journal, 29*(7), 1–12.

DeVault, M. L. (1990). Talking and listening from women's standpoint: Feminist strategies for interviewing and analysis. *Social Problems, 37*(1), 96–112.

DeVault, M. L. (1999). *Liberating method: Feminism and social research*. Philadelphia, PA: Temple University Press.

Dunlap, D. M., & Schmuck, P. A. (1995). *Women leading in education*. Albany, NY: State University of New York Press.

Eagly, A. H. (1987). *Sex differences in social behavior: A social-role interpretation*. Hillsdale, NJ: Erlbaum.

Eagly, A. H., & Carli, L. L. (2007). *Through the labyrinth: The truth about how women become leaders*. Cambridge, MA: Harvard Business School Press.

Eagly, A. H., & Johannesen-Schmidt, M. C. (2001). The leadership styles of women and men. *Journal of Social Issues, 57*(4), 781–797.

Eagly, A. H., Johannesen-Schmidt, M. C., & van Engen, M. L. (2003). Transformational, transactional, and laissez-faire leadership styles: A meta-analysis comparing women and men. *Psychological Bulletin*, *129*(4), 569–591.

Eagly, A. H., & Johnson, B. T. (1990). Gender and leadership style: A meta-analysis. *Psychological Bulletin*, *108*(2), 233–256.

Eagly, A. H., & Karau, S. J. (2002). Role congruity theory of prejudice toward female leaders. *Psychological Review*, *109*(3), 573–598.

Eisenhardt, K. M. (1989). Building theories from case study research. *The Academy of Management Review*, *14*(4), 532–550.

Ferree, M. M., & Purkayastha, B. (2000). Equality and cumulative disadvantage: Response to Baxter and Wright the glass ceiling hypothesis: A comparative study of the United States, Sweden, and Australia. *Gender & Society*, *14*(6), 809–813.

Fox, M. F. (2010). Women and men faculty in academic science and engineering: Social organizational indicators and implications. *American Behavioral Scientist*, *53*(7), 997–1012.

Gerson, K. (2010). *The unfinished revolution: Coming of age in a new era of gender, work, and family*. New York, NY: Oxford University Press.

Gibson, D. E. (2004). Role models in career development: New directions for theory and research. *Journal of Vocational Behavior*, *65*(1), 134–156.

Giroux, H., & Purpel, D. (1983). *The hidden curriculum and moral education*. Berkeley, CA: McCutchan.

Glaser, B., & Strauss, A. (1967). *The discovery of grounded theory*. Chicago, IL: Aldine Publishing Company.

Goodall, A. H. (2009). *Socrates in the boardroom: Why research universities should be led by top scholars*. Princeton, NJ: Princeton University Press.

Green, C. E., & King, V. G. (2001). Sisters mentoring sisters: Africentric leadership development for Black women in the academy. *The Journal of Negro Education, 70*(3), 156–165.

Haraway, D. (1991). A cyborg manifesto: Science, technology, and socialist-feminism in the late twentieth century. In. D. Haraway (Ed.), *Simians, cyborgs, and women* (pp. 149–181). New York, NY: Routledge.

Harding, S. (1986). The instability of the analytical categories of feminist theory. *Signs, 11*(4), 645–664.

Heilman, M. E., & Okimoto, T. G. (2007). Why are women penalized for success at male tasks? The implied communality deficit. *Journal of Applied Psychology, 92*(1), 81–92.

Helgesen, S. (1990). *The female advantage: Women's ways of leadership*. New York, NY: Doubleday Currency.

Hochschild, A. (1983). *The managed heart*. Berkeley, CA: University of California Press.

Hochschild, A. (1989). *The second shift*. New York, NY: Avon.

Hochschild, A. R. (1997). *The time bind: When work becomes home and home becomes work*. New York, NY: Metropolitan Books.

Jackson, P. W. (1990). *Life in classrooms*. New York, NY: Teachers College Press.

Jamieson, K. H. (1995). *Beyond the double bind: Women and leadership*. New York, NY: Oxford University Press.

Jaradat, M. H. (2013). The notion of administrative transparency among academic leaderships at Jordanian universities. *Education, 134*(1), 74–81.

Jones, S., Lefoe, G., Harvey, M., & Ryland, K. (2012). Distributed leadership: A collaborative framework for academics, executives and professionals in higher education. *Journal of Higher Education Policy and Management, 34*(1), 67–78.

Jung, J. (1986). How useful is the concept of a role model? A critical analysis. *Journal of Social Behavior & Personality, 1*(4), 525–536.

Kanter, R. M. (1977). *Men and women of the corporation*. New York, NY: Basic Books.

Kantola, J. (2008). Why do all the women disappear? Gendering processes in a political science department. *Gender, Work & Organization, 15*(2), 202–225.

Katila, S., & Eriksson, P. (2013). He is a firm, strong-minded and empowering leader, but is she? Gendered position of female and male CEOs. *Gender, Work & Organization, 20*(1), 71–84.

Kelly, E. L., Ammons, S. K, Chermack, K., & Moen, P. (2010). Gendered challenge, gendered response: Confronting the ideal worker norm in a white-collar organization. *Gender & Society, 24*(3), 281–303.

Keohane, N. O. (2010). *Thinking about leadership*. Princeton, NJ: Princeton University Press.

Kezar, A., Eckel, P., Contreras-McGavin, M., & Quaye, S. J. (2008). Creating a web of support: An important leadership strategy for advancing campus diversity. *Higher Education*, 55(1), 69–92.

Koenig, A. M., Eagly, A. H., Mitchell, A. A., & Ristikari, T. (2011). Are leader stereotypes masculine? A meta-analysis of three research paradigms. *Psychological Bulletin, 137*(4), 616–642.

Lakoff, R. T. (1975). *Language and women's place*. New York, NY: Harper & Row.

Langdon, E. A. (2001). Women's colleges then and now: Access then, equity now. *Peabody Journal of Education*, 76(1), 5–30.

Lewin, K., & Lippitt, R. (1938). An experimental approach to the study of autocracy and democracy: A preliminary note. *Sociometry, 1*, 292–300.

Lorber, J. (1984). *Women physicians: Careers, status, and power*. New York, NY: Routledge.

Lorber, J. (1994). *Paradoxes of gender*. New Haven, CT: Yale University Press.

Lorber, J. (2000). Using gender to undo gender: A feminist degendering movement. *Feminist Theory, 1*(1), 79–95.

Lorber, J. (2005). *Breaking the bowls: Degendering and feminist change*. New York, NY: W.W. Norton.

Lovejoy, M., & Stone, P. (2012). Opting back in: The influence of time at home on professional women's career redirection after opting out. *Gender, Work & Organization, 19*(6), 631–653.

Macdonald, C. L. (2010). *Shadow mothers: Nannies, au pairs, and the micropolitics of mothering*. Berkeley, CA: University of California Press.

Mahoney, P. (1998). Democracy and school leadership in England and Denmark. *British Journal of Educational Studies, 46*(3), 302–317.

Margolis, E., & Romero, M. (1998). The department is very male, very white, very old, and very conservative: The functioning of the hidden curriculum in graduate sociology departments. *Harvard Educational Review, 68*(1), 1–33.

Martin, A. J., & Dowson, M. (2009). Interpersonal relationships, motivation, engagement, and achievement: Yields for theory, current issues, and educational practice. *Review of Educational Research, 79*(1), 327–365.

Martin, P. Y. (2001). 'Mobilizing masculinities': Women's experiences of men at work. *Organization, 8*(4), 587–618.

Martin, P. Y. (2003). "Said and done" vs. "saying and doing": Gendering practices, practicing *gender at work*. *Gender & Society, 17*(3), 342–366.

McFarland, D. A., & Thomas, R. J. (2006). Bowling young: How youth voluntary associations influence adult political participation. *American Sociological Review, 71*(3), 401–425.

McLaughlin, H., Uggen, C., & Blackstone, A. (2012). Sexual harassment, workplace authority, and the paradox of power. *American Sociological Review, 77*(4), 625–647.

Merton, R. K. (1968). *Social theory and social structure* (Rev. ed.). New York, NY: Free Press.

Mills, C. W. (1956). *The power elite*. Oxford: Oxford University Press.

Morgan, L. A., & Martin, K. A. (2006). Taking women professionals out of the office: The case of women in sales. *Gender & Society*, *20*(1), 108–128.

Muhr, S. L. (2011). Caught in the gendered machine: On the masculine and feminine in cyborg leadership. *Gender, Work & Organization*, *18*(3), 337–357.

Naples, N. A. (2003). *Ethnography, discourse analysis, and activist research*. New York, NY: Routledge.

Ollilainen, M., & Calasanti, T. (2007). Metaphors at work: Maintaining the salience of gender in self-managing teams. *Gender & Society*, 21(1), 5–27.

Pascale, C. (2007). *Making sense of race, class, and gender: Commonsense, power, and privilege in the United States*. New York, NY: Routledge.

Petev, I. D. (2013). The association of social class and lifestyles: Persistence in American sociability, 1974–2010. *American Sociological Review,* 78(4), 633–661.

Pierce, J. L. (1995). *Gender trials: Emotional lives in contemporary law firms*. Berkeley, CA: University of California Press.

Pierce, J. L. (2003). Traveling from feminism to mainstream sociology and back: One woman's tale of tenure and the politics of backlash. *Qualitative Sociology*, 26(3), 369–396.

Pini, B. (2005). The third sex: Women leaders in Australian agriculture. *Gender, Work & Organization*, *12*(1), 73–88.

Plucker, J. A. (1998). The relationship between school climate conditions and student aspirations. *The Journal of Educational Research*, 91(4), 240–246.

Ridgeway, C. L. (1997). Interaction and the conservation of gender inequality: Considering employment. *American Sociological Review, 62*(2), 218–235.

Ridgeway, C. (2001). Gender, status, and leadership. *Journal of Social Issues, 57*(4), 637–655.

Rosenthal, C. S. (1998). *When women lead: Integrative leadership in state legislatures*. New York, NY: Oxford University Press.

Rowley, J. (1997). Academic leaders: Made or born? *Industrial and Commercial Training, 29*, 78–84.

Scandura, T. A., & Schriesheim, C. A. (1994). Leader-member exchange and supervisor career mentoring as complementary constructs in leadership research. *The Academy of Management Journal, 37*(6), 1588–1602.

Schull, V., Shaw, S., & Kihl, L. A. (2013). If a woman came in … she would have been eaten up alive: Analyzing gendered political processes in the search for an athletic director. *Gender & Society, 27*(1), 56–81.

Smidt, C. (1980). Civil religious orientations among elementary school children. *Sociology of Religion, 41*(1), 25–40.

Smith, D. (2005). *Institutional ethnography: A sociology for people*. Walnut Grove, CA: AltaMira Press.

Smith, D. E. (1987). *The everyday world as problematic: A feminist sociology*. Boston, MA: Northeastern University Press.

Spence, J. T., & Buckner, C. E. (2000). Instrumental and expressive traits, trait stereotypes, and sexist attitudes. *Psychology of Women Quarterly, 24*(1), 44–62.

Sprague, J. (2005). *Feminist methodologies for critical researchers: Bridging differences*. Walnut Creek, CA: Rowman & Littlefield.

Suarez-Mccrink, C. (2002). Hispanic women: Building a room for self-efficacy. *Journal of Hispanic Higher Education*, *1*(3), 238–250.

Thomas, G. (2011). Michelle Bachelet's liderazgo femenino (feminine leadership): Redefining political leadership in Chile's 2005 presidential campaign. *International Feminist Journal of Politics*, *13*(1), 63–82.

Thomson, E., & McLanahan, S. S. (2012). Reflections on family structure and child well-being: Economic resources vs. parental socialization. *Social Forces*, *91*(1), 45–53.

Tuchman, G. (2009). *Wannabe U: Inside the corporate university*. Chicago, IL: University of Chicago Press.

Uk Chun, J., Sosik, J. J., & Yun, N. Y. (2012). A longitudinal study of mentor and protégé outcomes in formal mentoring relationships. *Journal of Organizational Behavior*, *33*(8), 1071–1094.

Valian, V. (2004). Beyond gender schemas: Improving the advancement of women in academia. *NWSA Journal*, *16*, 207–220.

van Ameijde, J. D. J., Nelson, P. C., Billsberry, J., & van Meurs, N. (2009). Improving leadership in higher education institutions: A distributed perspective. *Higher Education*, *58*(6), 763–779.

Wass, V., & McNabb, R. (2006). Pay, promotion and parenthood amongst women solicitors. *Work, Employment & Society*, *20*(2), 289–308.

Williams, C. (1992). The glass escalator—Hidden advantages for men in female professions. *Social Problems*, *39*(3), 253–267.

Williams, C. (1995). *Still a man's world*. Berkeley, CA: University of California Press.

Williams, J. C. (2010). *Reshaping the work–family debate: Why men and class matter*. Cambridge, MA: Harvard University Press.

Williams, K. (1989). Researching the powerful: Problems and possibilities of social research. *Crime, Law and Social Change*, *13*(3), 253–274.

Williams, P. (1991). *The alchemy of race and rights: Diary of a law professor*. Cambridge, MA: Harvard University Press.

Zippel, K. S. (2006). *The politics of sexual harassment: A comparative study of the United States, the European Union, and Germany*. Cambridge: Cambridge University Press.

Zweigenhaft, R. L. & Domhoff, G. W. (2006). *Diversity in the power elite: How it happened, why it matters*. Lanham, MD: Rowman & Littlefield.

INDEX

Note: Page numbers followed by "*n*" with numbers indicate notes.

Academic leadership, 20, 36, 63, 149
   benefits of formal leadership training, 91–97
   early pathway to academic leadership and mentors, 63–64
   effective, 150
   faculty/administrator experience, 67–70
   formal leadership training, 91
   impossibility of gender blindness in, 153
   learning from others' leadership style, 71–78
   learning from successes and mistakes of others and self, 70–71
   listening and learning to lead, 89–90
   muddling through and learning on-the-job, 82–86
   narratives, 149
   non-role model, 78–82
   predecessors, 87–89
   roles, 27
   suggestions for future research, 154
   training for women, 98–108
   undergraduate and graduate school experience, 64–67
   women advance to, 151
Advantages, 141–146
Age, 137–138, 152
Agentic approach, 55–56
Agentic leadership, 6
American Council on Education (ACE), 2, 101
Arts and Sciences (A&S), 10

Index

Association of Governing Boards of Universities and Colleges (AGB), 108*n*2
Authentic leadership, 76
Authoritarian, 6, 131
Authority, questioning of, 122–131
Autocratic leadership style, 5

Bachelet's strategy, 16
Board of Trustees, 31, 35, 73, 130, 154

Campus-wide emergencies, 19
"Career academic", 36
Career-minded university leader, 38
Careerism/careerist, 37–38
 agendas, 38
 persona, 38
Caring for institution, 36–38
Children, 115–118, 120–121, 152
Cisgender, 8
Class, 13, 26, 149, 154
Close/distant role modeling, 70
Collaboration, 5, 21, 57, 64
Collaborative leadership style, 55
Communal leadership, 6
 style, 55

Communal/agentic leadership style, 6
Corporate, 8, 19
 administrators, 20
 contracts, 27
Credentials, exceptional academic, 20–31
Cultural respect, 31–36
Culture, 20, 31–33, 61, 123, 150
Cyborg, 147*n*1

Dean, 59
Degendering leadership, 2, 4
Democratic engagement, 5, 31
Democratic leadership style, 4–5, 15
Disciplinary diversity, 54, 56
Disciplinary homes, 10
Discourse analysis, 14
Diversity, 2, 8–10, 17, 20, 46–55
Double bind, 122

Earning citizenship, 31
Education, 10
 scholars, 46–47
Effective academic leadership, 19–20
 caring for institution, 36–38
 exceptional academic credentials, 20–36
 hail to position, 39–43
 leading with ego, 31–36

personnel issues, 43–46
teamwork, 55–61
valuing diversity of opinions, 46–55
Effective leadership, 42, 52, 59, 61
Ego, leading with, 31–36
Emotional labor, 7, 111
Essentialism, gender, 1, 17, 107
Ethnicity, 2, 107–108, 149, 153–154
Exceptional academic credentials, 20
academic leadership, 21–22
academic training, 27–28
changing landscape, 28–29
Earning citizenship, 31
faculty members, 20–21
leadership hierarchy, 23–24
leadership role, 24–25
teaching, 25–26
university leadership, 30

Faculty/administrator experience of academic leadership, 67–70
Family balance, 114–122
Family-related matters, 121
Feminine, 1
leadership, 17
Femininity, 16, 147*n*1
Feminist degendering movement, 4

Formal leadership training, 91
benefits, 91–97

Gender, 122, 152
binary, 1
essentialism, 1
gender-based differences, 150
gender-based harassment, 136–138
gender-based mentoring, 144
leadership styles and, 15–18
roles, 151
trials, 123
Gender-specific leadership trainings, 98, 144, 150–151
Gendered advantages, 141–146
Gendered democratic/authoritarian leadership style, 6
Gendered imbalance, 120
Gendered leadership, 3, 5, 15, 153
Glass ceiling, 2, 141–146
Glass escalator, 142, 147*n*3
Global/specific role modeling, 70
Graduate school experience, 64–67
Grounded theory approach, 13

Index

Hands-off approach, 6
Harassment
  sexual, 122, 136–137, 141
  workplace, 136–141
Hidden power dimensions, 14
Hierarchy, leadership, 23–24
Higher education, gender and leadership in, 109
  gender and power, 122
  power trips, 131–136
  questioning of authority, 122–131
  socially constructed gendered leadership gender roles, 110–114
  work and family balance, 114–122
Higher Education Resource Services (HERS), 99–100, 102, 104

Individual leadership approaches, 1
Institutional culture, 34–35
Institutional stakeholders, 20
Intersex leadership, 1–2, 153

Labor-intensive employment, 152
Laissez-faire leadership, 5

Laissez-faire style, 6
Leader(ship), 17, 36, 39, 40, 58, 57, 108
  degendering, 2
  disciplinary, 10–12
  efficacy, 149–150
  in gender-neutral terms, 2–3
  hidden power dimensions, 14
  lack of diversity, 8–9
  relations of ruling, 7–8
  scholars, 5, 46–47
  sociology for people, 13
  STEM, 9–10
  study design, 7
  styles and gender, 15–18
  theorizing leadership variation, 4–7
  trainings, 97
Leadership style, 6–7, 13, 78–79, 133–134
  learning from others, 71–78
Leading with ego, 31–36
Learning
  to lead, 89–90
  leadership assessment, 83
  from mistakes, 78–82
  on-the-job, 82–86
Liderazgo feminino (Feminine leadership), 16
Listening to lead, 89–90
Literary disciplinary, 54

Masculine/masculinity, 1, 16–17, 147*n*1
Mentoring, 7, 38, 42, 58, 64, 67–69, 82, 106, 150
Mentors, 69–70
  early pathway to, 63–64
Mentorship, 68, 70
Military, 9
Mistakes
  learning from, 78–82, 150
  others and self, 70–71

Networking, 92, 93, 102, 104, 107
Non-binary, 1–2, 17
Non-cis-gender leaders, 146
Non-discrimination policy, 33
Non-role models, 78–82
Nurturing future leaders, 58

"On-the-job" learning, 150
Open in-person dialogues, 48
Openness, 5

Parents, 85–86
Path, 31, 64, 66, 91, 104, 135, 149, 154
Patriarchy, 9
Peer groups, 63
Ph. D. (doctorate), 25–26, 28
Politics, 16–17, 33, 76

Positive/negative role modeling, 70
Power, 122, 152
  trips, 131–136
Predecessors, 87–89
Problem-solving process, 129

Race, 2, 8, 13–14, 46, 107–108, 149, 153–154
Religion, 33, 63, 153
Research (scholarship), 24, 82, 103
Respondents, 152
Role models, 70

"Second shift" labor, 118
Sexual harassment, 122, 128, 136–137, 141
Sexuality, 2, 8, 13, 107, 149, 153–154
Shared governance, 5–6, 19, 55–57, 103, 123, 150
Social media, 48–49
Social role theory, 5, 15
Socialization, 63, 67, 103
Socially constructed gendered leadership gender roles, 110–114
Sports-themed Barbie, 16
Stakeholders, 113, 152
STEM (Science, Technology, Engineering, and Mathematics), 9, 98, 142

Stereotypes, 153
Students, 9, 26, 31, 33, 46–51, 56, 64, 85, 126
Successes, 70–71, 106–107, 150
Successor, 39, 87–89

Teaching, 21, 23–25, 38, 91, 96
Team diversity, 54–55
Teamwork, 55–61
Theorizing leadership variation, 4–7
Time-consuming leadership role, 119–120
Training for women, 98–108
Trans/transgender, 1, 17, 153
Transactional approach, 6–7
Transactional leadership, 5–7
Transformational leadership, 5–7
Transparency, 5

Undergraduate school experience, 64–67

Valuing diversity of opinions, 46
  administrators, 46–47
  deal with situation, 50–51
  effective leader role, 52
  openness, 48
  quality, 52–53
  social media, 48–49
  team diversity, 54–55

Woman leadership, 1
Women respondents, 114–115
  respondents, 119
  training for, 98–108
Work and family balance, 114–122
Workplace harassment, 136–141

Printed in the United States
By Bookmasters